GW00771279

To/ Vice Admiral Sir Louis Le Bailly.
With Best Wishes & very many thanks

Peter Gibbings

WEEP FOR ME, COMRADE

Peter Gibbings

MINERVA PRESS
LONDON
MONTREUX LOS ANGELES SYDNEY

WEEP FOR ME, COMRADE

ISBN 1 86106 437 3

First Published 1997 by
MINERVA PRESS
195 Knightsbridge
London SW7 1RE

Printed in Great Britain by
Antony Rowe Ltd, Chippenham, Wiltshire

WEEP FOR ME, COMRADE

Dedication

To the memory of my father who lost his life in HMS *Courageous* and my dear mother; one of the first widows of that terrible war who lived up to the name of that ship, and was truly courageous.

About the Author

Peter Gibbings was born in Plymouth where he spent his early years. His father was a Petty Officer in the Royal Navy, and his mother a nurse. The family moved to London when his father pensioned from the navy, and he continued his education at Stag Lane primary school, Edgeware, and after his father's death, at the royal hospital school, Holbrook, in Suffolk. He entered the Royal Navy as a sick berth attendant in 1946 and trained at the Royal Naval Hospital, Stonehouse, Plymouth, after which he served in the third destroyer flotilla in the Mediterranean until medically discharged from the Royal Navy in 1949. He then trained as a chiropodist and qualified in 1951 and set up in Plymouth, and practised there for over forty years. Since his retirement, he has lived with his wife, Doris, in the village of Walkhampton, on the edge of Dartmoor. They have a son, a daughter, and eight grandchildren. His main interests are the Royal Navy, and anything to do with ships and the sea. He has a lifelong love of music, and after retiring took up the trombone which he plays for the Plymouth Royal Navy Volunteer Band. In recent years he has given considerable time to the study of naval matters; particularly the cutbacks in the armed services and the dismantling of training capacity and facilities, believing that history is repeating itself, and that the resulting inability of services to cope with anything more than minor world conflagrations gives rise to serious concern. His other interests are painting (maritime and seascape), reading, and tending a very large garden with his wife.

Thanks

The author wishes to thank Lieutenant Mike Jepp RN for his work in translating Kapt. Schuhart's log covering the sinking of HMS *Courageous*.

Foreword

By Vice Admiral Sir Louis Le Bailly, KBE, CB, DL

I suppose there are not very many of us left who recall the shock when HMS *Courageous*, one of the then Navy's only five aircraft carriers, was sunk just fourteen days after World War II started. And it was common knowledge that just four days before, HMS *Ark Royal*, another of the five, had been near missed by two torpedoes. Nine days later *Ark Royal* was near missed again, this time by bombs, and HMS *Hood* was hard hit by a bomb in the same attack.

Peter Gibbings was approaching his eleventh birthday when his father, a chief petty officer cook, having retired after twenty-two years' service, was recalled to join Devonport based *Courageous* at the end of her refit in July 1939. Devonport had been his home port and like so many who have left the Navy at the end of their 'time' he had become a real strength to the community. Having entered the civil service his new salary, added to a well-earned if meagre naval pension, allowed the Gibbings family to start buying a house with a large garden in a desirable part of London, and generally begin to prosper; to become, as Peter's father described them, Mr and Mrs Suburbia. Then, thanks to Hitler, all this had to be put on to temporary 'hold' while Mrs Gibbings and her family migrated to their old stamping ground, Devonport, to be near Mr, now once more, Chief Petty Officer Gibbings.

Courageous was commissioned just a month before war was declared; one third of the ship's company were reservists or newly fledged sailors. Like *Ark Royal* and HMS *Hermes*, her first (and last) operational role was, with a small destroyer escort and notably ephemeral Rules of Engagement, to hunt German submarines (on station since mid-August) off the Western Approaches. That, then, is the background to this story told by Chief Petty Officer Gibbings' naval son.

In a rather 'scatter-gun' approach, Peter Gibbings covers several fields of abiding interest: descriptions of the captains of *Courageous*, and U29 who torpedoed her, with the latter's log for the day of the attack; accounts of the small proportion of the ship's company who were fortunate enough to survive and of the tragic loss of the many whom the nation, let alone the Navy, could ill afford to lose. But Peter Gibbings poses broader questions. How was it that, after the Munich warning, the Navy and the country was still so ill prepared? (I recall a lecture to officers in Portsmouth in April 1939 by Professor Lewis Namier, in which he forecast war during the first week in September, and the almost contemptuous riposte by the senior officer present.) How was it that the majority of *Courageous*' ships company had no lifebelts, and this only two decades from World War I? How was it that after a refit many of *Courageous*' Carley floats were still so painted up that they could not be released, or that the electrical ring main could not be subdivided? How was it that there was no guidance as to which side of a sinking ship the survivors should take to the water? (There was still no guidance two and a half years later when my own ship was sunk.)

It is from those terrible omissions that Peter Gibbings issues a warning about what is happening today. The Royal Navy is at its lowest manpower strength since the aftermath of the Peace of Amiens two centuries ago. The abandonment, due to political pressure and falsified naval data, of the Royal Naval Engineering College at Manadon, newly built in order, from lessons derived in World War II, to resurrect Admiral Fisher's dictum that *all* officers should be trained "up to a certain point [with] some community of technical knowledge and a lifelong community of sentiment".

But Gibbings' most explosive salvo is "to go beyond the pain, struggle and sacrifice of those involved at the sharp end of the war and follow what happens to those left behind: the widows, orphans, fathers, mothers, brothers and sisters; to highlight the shameful way that successive governments have treated the war widow and the war orphan, the war disabled and veterans of our country, and to compare their treatment with that of other nations towards their people, including our defeated enemies."

In small ways things have improved of course. After *Courageous* was sunk, Gibbings' mother stood with other next of kin, in the cold outside the gates of Devonport Barracks, greeting the few survivors and asking for news, and waiting, and waiting, until late on the third day, a kindly chief petty officer came out to tell the smaller crowd "that there were no more survivors". The Navy did things better in the Falklands War but the shameful treatment of the widows of World Wars I and II remains a blot on the nation's heritage, for which successive politicians should have been, and should still be, impeached.

From the days of King Alfred to the Falklands and Gulf wars, the Royal Navy, consistently starved in peacetime, has never let the nation down. *Weep For Me, Comrade* should remind us of how our fighting men of all three services have dragged our country out of the pit into which supine political manoeuvring has time and again condemned it.

"The man of character in peace is the man of courage in war." So wrote Lord Moran of his experience in the trenches in World War I, and as Churchill's physician in World War II. The services select boys of character and build them into something which too many in civil life, especially when war is not imminent, come to dislike, if not sometimes even to despise.

The song sung by the Royal Australian Navy seems an apt tribute to the memory of Chief Petty Officer Gibbings and to his brave widow, as well as to the author:

Fair is the fame of our fathers who fought for us
Over the mainland and out on the foam;
Shall we not cling to the heritage bought for us
Shoulder the burden, hold to our home?

So when the shadow shall fall on the way of us
Nearing the goal of our three score and ten,
Haply our sons and their children may say of us –
These have been faithful, these have been men.

Contents

Prologue

This is the story of the death of a ship, and many of the men who served in her. It is pieced together from the official reports available at the time of writing; statements from all the survivors that I could trace; from the war diary of the commander of the U-boat responsible for her sinking, U29; correspondence between myself and the commander, Kapitanleutnant Otto Schuhart, later Kapitan Zur See retired, and from a meeting with him when he kindly allowed me to visit him at his home in Stuttgart. All the details that led up to the sinking, i.e. the movements, positions, course, speed and signals, received and sent, are from archives or archive documents, and statements taken from those who were concerned.

The reader may well ask, why, after all this time, should there be any need for another war book? Haven't there been enough; indeed too many? I can only answer that if it was intended to be just another war book, then, perhaps yes. Indeed, one survivor wrote: "*Courageous* was not the only ship wasted, merely the first." He was, of course, right. So many good ships and fine men followed all too quickly, and 'wasted' was indeed the operative word. But of course, the answer is no.

There are two main characters in this story. The first is Captain W T Makeig-Jones RN. I had the pleasure of meeting his nearest surviving relative, his nephew, Col. Makeig-Jones, Ret'd, when he and his wife kindly invited my wife and I to have lunch with them, following my request for information about the captain. This has enabled me to form a mental picture of this fine man, a picture which has been verified by the few men of *Courageous* who knew him as their commanding officer in the so very short time that the ship's company had to get to know each other before her end.

The other is Kapitanleutnant Otto Schuhart, who commanded U29 when she met and sank *Courageous*. He was most kind in answering my many questions, both in writing and when we met, which was at times very difficult for him, owing to my lack of knowledge of the German language.

When I first contacted Kapitanleutnant Schuhart, I asked him what feelings went through his mind at that time. He replied: "I was a soldier, I had no enthusiasm for war, nor had I sentiments of hate towards my adversary. I loved my country and had to do my duty."

Always in September my mind goes back to the beginning of the war and the period that led up to it. It is something that I will never forget while I draw breath: 1938, when my father was recalled from pension, and demobilised when Chamberlain waved his pathetic piece of paper and said: "Peace in our time".

I can never suppose that he was so naïve as to believe that it was really going to buy us enough time to stem the disaster which had stared Europe in the face for many years. I remember again 1939, when my father was called back for a second time into the service. I remember so vividly hearing the declaration of war and the first air raid warning. We lived in London at the time, where my father worked in the General Post Office, after taking his pension from the Navy.

At that time, as a boy of ten, I didn't realise the enormity of what had happened. I remember seeing the film *All Quiet on the Western Front* at the Plaza Cinema in Queensbury, Middlesex, on the Saturday of the weekend of the Munich crisis, and not understanding its message. To me, war was something exciting, the killing unreal as in our children's games, "Bang, bang, you're dead". When the war became a reality in 1939 it still made only a slight impression on me. How soon all that was to change.

Self-criticism has always been one of our assets as a nation, and another is probably our sense of humour. But history is strewn with occasions when we had the sense to be self-critical, and the stupidity to laugh it off.

All through history, the defences of this country have only been strengthened when war came, and only rarely before it. Indeed, there has always been a reluctance to spend money on armaments at any time. This reluctance can be understood when the threat of war recedes into the background, but surely it can never be understood or forgiven when all the warning signs are present. Never was this more true than in the years from the time when Adolf Hitler came to power to the time of the outbreak of war.

No man goes through life without making mistakes. But there are times when some men make mistakes of such magnitude as to render them unfit to occupy positions of high responsibility any longer. Such were many of the men in political life of this country between the two world wars, who, ignoring all the danger signs and warnings, led (if such a word can be used in this context) this country into a war for which we were in no way prepared, either politically, economically or militarily.

Between the wars, self-seeking politicians, eager to gain power and cheap popularity, clamoured for disarmament and the reduction of the armed forces, and failed to update our weaponry and defence systems, in the face of growing threats from the enemies of civilisation. Yet these men, when faced eventually by the inevitable result of their folly, and in some cases cupidity, were the most vociferous in laying the blame for the resultant military disasters at the door of those at the sharp end, who very often had been courageous enough to speak out and oppose them.

There can be little doubt that the Second World War had its roots in the Versailles Treaty, which was conceived as much out of vengeance and spite as out of necessity. Although it is not the purpose of this book to argue this point, it is stated if for no other reason than to show that it is never wise in any dispute to push your opponent into a corner so tight that he has no option but to come out fighting. At the very least it gave Hitler grist for his mill. How well he used it!

It can be said that we are all wise with hindsight, but the blindness of government in the 1930s was monumental and could only be described as ostrich-like. It is easy to understand that war-weariness on the part of the protagonists lulled us into a false sense of security. "Never again" was written on many war memorials, and without doubt was genuinely meant. For many years nobody believed that either side would ever indulge in such madness again. But from the early thirties it was clear that something intensely evil was stirring in Europe, and it became more obvious as time went on, until 1933, when it was too late to stop it, unless we showed determination that we could, and would.

There is another purpose of this book. It is to do something which I do not feel has been adequately done elsewhere. That is, to try and go beyond the pain, struggle and sacrifice of those involved at the sharp end of the war and follow what happens to those left behind: the widows, orphans, fathers, mothers, brothers and sisters; to highlight the shameful way that successive governments have treated the war widow and the war orphan, the war disabled and veterans of our country, and to compare their treatment with that of other nations towards their people, including our defeated enemies.

When on Remembrance Sunday each year politicians stand before the Cenotaph, their eyes must be blind if their consciences are not affected by the words so plainly and poignantly written on Lutyens memorial: "LEST WE FORGET". Conveniently, they have never remembered. It is now over fifty years since the end of the last war, and there are not all that many widows and disabled left, but the few that are still with us now need help in their declining years. The cost would be so small, and the debt is so long overdue. To compound the already massive insult, the widows of the 1939-45 conflict lag light years behind those of our late enemies. Also, they are not given anywhere near as much as the widows of servicemen who gave their lives in Aden, the Falklands, Iraq, and Northern Ireland. In short, the widows of all servicemen after 1973 receive vastly more than their 1939-45 sisters. Perhaps the 1939 war victims are not quite so dead, and their widows don't get quite so cold or as hungry, and get reduced rent and free clothing. It doesn't take a genius to know that the needs of old age are greater, and income smaller. This anomaly is a disgrace to our otherwise great nation. It is time to end this glaring injustice.

It is interesting to note that if a war widow remarried, she was given a year's pension as a dowry. One can be forgiven for thinking, 'Cheap at the price'. When a man was recalled from pension and killed in warfare, the government lost very little. The pension paid to his widow would have been paid to him had he lived. My father's life cost his country nothing. How cheap is human life.

Weep for Me, Comrade

Weep for me, comrade, for my untimely end.
My hopes and dreams all unfulfilled will be.
For loved ones, show the care I cannot send,
and try to ease their pain for me.
The time that stopped for me goes lonely on for them
until they learn the thread of life to take,
and onward go, with courage, for my sake.

Aye, my comrade, weep for thee I will.
That you are gone, and I remain to tell the world thy fears.
But time has passed; the world no longer wants to know,
and so, for you I'll dry my tears.
A watchful eye on those you love I'll keep.
Instead of you, for them I'll weep.

P.E.Gibbings

Chapter One

A Lesson not Learned

In the First World War, Britain was nearly brought to her knees by the highly successful U-boat campaign waged by Germany. One would have thought that such a terrible lesson would never have been forgotten by the politicians and those holding high office in the Navy, but history proved that their ability to learn from such narrowly averted tragedy was less than that of a ten-year-old child.

On 1st April 1918, appropriately All Fools' Day, the Royal Naval Air Service and the Royal Flying Corps merged to form the Royal Air Force. It was from this time that the rot set in for naval flying. It defies understanding that the very service which was the main instrument in defeating the U-boat in the First World War was almost destroyed, and the majority of its most capable personnel transferred to the newly-formed RAF, leaving behind men who in most cases were demoralised and could be forgiven for thinking that what was left was a side-show and a sop to the concept of naval aviation. Winston Churchill argued for the return of control of naval aviation in 1936, and it was only slowly that these grave errors were recognised and some steps were taken to mitigate the damage. There was very little money to be spared for the Armed Forces between the wars, and consequently the clawing back of control of naval aviation was a slow and piecemeal process. It was Churchill who eventually tipped the scales with his support of Lord Chatfield, the First Sea Lord, who threatened to resign if the control of naval aviation was not returned to the Navy.

The lead in naval aviation built up by Britain was very quickly dissipated after the end of WWI, and inter-service rivalry, which played no small part in the débâcle, was compounded by the fact that the whole of naval aviation was in the hands of the RAF, which had no clear idea of the aviation requirements of the RN. It was not until

1921 that the first concession was made – that naval officers could be trained as observers; but it was not until 1923 that a committee of enquiry recommended that all observers in RN aircraft should be naval officers and up to 70% of pilots should be naval officers with dual RAF rank, and in 1924 the carrier-borne branch of the RAF became the FAA.

It was not until 1936 that matters really came to a head, when the First Sea Lord, Admiral Chatfield, determined to bring about the complete control of the FAA by making it a resignation issue. In this he was backed by Winston Churchill, whose voice had over the years been raised in warning about the dangers of ignoring Nazi dictatorship and overt rearmament. It was only this that brought a reluctant government to its senses, if only to a minimal extent, and it was not until July 1937 that the Admiralty regained full control of naval aviation; but as can be seen from the account of the sinking of *Courageous*, there were many RAF personnel aboard her two full years after.

This amply demonstrates that the training of many of the FAA officers and men was still not fully developed, and certainly the incomplete training of observers was a cogent factor in the sinking of *Courageous*, and was recognised as such by the Board of Enquiry.

The Royal Navy entered the war with seven aircraft-carriers. To take them in order of their appearance on the scene of naval aviation, the first true carrier was *Argus*, which was laid down by Beardmore as a liner, the *Conte Rosso*, for an Italian shipping company in 1914, purchased for the Navy in 1916, and completed as a carrier in 1918 from a design drawn up in 1912. Because of problems arising from hot furnace gases from the funnel of *Argus* when she was in her experimental role in 1916, she was given a clear flight deck over her complete length, and furnace smoke and gases were extracted via fans through horizontal smoke ducts which opened out aft. She was affectionately known in the service as the "floating ditty-box". Although she was not the first purpose-built carrier, she was the first to have been built from the hull up. Whilst there had been numerous experiments carried out with seaplane carriers and the launching of aircraft from gun platforms, this was the first attempt at a real carrier.

In 1937 *Argus* was converted to the handling and maintenance of radio-controlled aircraft and lost nearly all her armament in 1939. During the war, she was mainly used as a ferrying carrier.

Hermes was next. She was the first carrier in the world to be purpose-built from the keel up. Built by the Armstrong Yard, she was launched in 1919 and completed at Devonport in 1923, and although the smallest of the type, it was she who really set the seal on future carrier design.

Eagle, although laid down by the Armstrong Yard in 1913 as a battleship for Chile, the *Almirante Cochrane*, remained on the stocks until 1917, when she was purchased and converted into a carrier, and although she was completed for her preliminary trials she was not commissioned until 1924.

Chapter Two

Courageous

Courageous, *Glorious* and *Furious* were the brainchildren of Admiral Sir John ('Jacky') Fisher, who before the First World War envisaged that in the event of war there would probably be need of vessels for operations in the Baltic, with heavy fire power but shallow draught. The resulting vessels can only be described as hybrid or hermaphrodite - indeed, they were once referred to as the "Curious", "Spurious" and "Erroneous".

Courageous and *Furious* were built at the Armstrong Yard, and the *Glorious* by Harland & Wolf, and although they were officially described as battle cruisers, Fisher's own description of them was large light cruisers, and although *Courageous* and *Glorious* each had four 15" guns, and *Furious* two 18", they were very scantily armoured. All three of these ships were extremely fast. The author was informed by one of her engineer officers that *Courageous* was capable of thirty-two knots "with all eighteen kettles going". Indeed, she had once beaten the *Queen Mary*'s time for an Atlantic crossing.

The vessels were nevertheless of little use in their original form, because the purpose for which they were built, i.e. landings in the Baltic, never materialised, and no other useful purpose could be found for such lightly armoured large ships.

Furious was converted into a hybrid aircraft-carrier before completion, with a flight deck forward, and was later completely converted.

Courageous was taken in hand in June 1924 for conversion into an aircraft-carrier designed to carry fifty aircraft, and was completed in May 1928. The results were not altogether unsuccessful, and apart from details, the basic design of aircraft-carriers has not changed very much from that time.

Courageous led a very busy life from the time of her conversion, and she was seldom idle. She contributed in no small way to the development of naval aviation in the days of austerity between the wars, when government folly reduced the size and effectiveness of all branches of the service, including the Fleet Air Arm. Even during the time when war was inevitable, the Admiralty treated naval aviation as very much a poor relation. The fact that aviation in the Royal Navy managed to cling on by its fingernails was only due to the dedication and foresight of many of its junior officers at the sharp end. They often had to force innovations and techniques through to the attention of those above, who more often than not adopted the ostrich posture. Nearly all the advances made in naval aviation were made despite those at the top, and only rarely because of them.

Finally, the *Ark Royal*. She, like *Hermes*, was purpose-built with the benefit of all the experience gained in building and converting all the others, and was the forerunner of a general concept for the carriers to follow in the Second World War, a concept which altered very little until the present generation. Laid down by Cammell Laird in 1935, she was launched in 1937 and completed in 1938.

These then were the seven carriers with which Britain entered the war. All except *Ark Royal* were between twenty and twenty-two years old, four of them converted battleships and the other built up from a liner hull, and could not be considered as a front line carrier. Other factors which had a great bearing on our plight at the outbreak of war included, of course, the Washington Naval Treaty of 1921, which resulted in our voluntarily limiting the building and displacement of our ships, and the scrapping of some others. But Germany, which was not bound by the Treaty, was free to build capital ships which exceeded ours in displacement by 10-15000 tons. This resulted in the building of the *Bismarck* and *Turpitz*, which, unlike our capital ships, did not have to sacrifice armour for firepower.

In addition to this, we suffered from a self-inflicted wound, Geddes' Axe, which was the result of a report by the Committee on National Expenditure, which was chaired by Sir Eric Geddes, published on 10th February 1922, and dealt with the armed and social services. About a quarter of it was devoted to a critical examination of the Navy estimates. The conclusion of the report was that there was an excess of over 33,000 officers and men in the Navy (nearly three-quarters of our present navy manpower), and eventually recommended a reduction of 35,000 men, and a reduction in the number of fighting ships, which they considered to be in excess of the requirement to meet the defence needs at that time. This resulted in many of our most able officers and men having their naval careers cut short and leaving the service. Some of the more fortunate managed to find employment in the merchant service in various shipping lines. Those who were less fortunate managed to find some sort of work, but often unrelated to the sea. All of them, to a greater or lesser extent, lost the sharp edge of their skills - skills which both they and the nation were shortly going to need very badly.

The last factor in the long catalogue of neglect and incompetence was the abolition as a post-war economy of the anti-submarine division of the naval staff, which was only re-established in the autumn of 1939. A lesson not learned, then, is repeating itself even now. Please God may we learn it in time. If we don't, the next generation may have to pick up the tab. Those who do not learn the lessons of history are destined to relive them.

Absolution

A hundred metres 'neath the waves I wait
to kill, or failing, meet my fate.
My nerves are tense, my senses are alert.
I pray; my eyes to heaven I avert.

We both are hunters, you and I.
We both must kill, or else we die.
What drives us on, each other to destroy?
Your death could never give me joy.

And yet unceasingly I try,
to kill you, never knowing why.
Each knows that only one can live.
Whichever one, the other must forgive.

P.E. Gibbings

Chapter Three

U29

U29 was a type 7A boat of which ten were built (U27-U36). She was built at the A.G. Weser shipyard in Bremen in 1936.

She had a complement of thirty-eight: four officers, three chief petty officers, twelve NCOs and nineteen seamen, all of whom were aged between twenty-one and thirty and all regular service. Submarines had no reservists with the exception of lieutenants second class, and a very small number of captains in the latter part of the war.

Her displacement was 915/1070 tons, her speed on the surface was 16-17 Kts, and her armament consisted of one 8.8cm gun and one 3.7cm anti-aircraft gun. She had five torpedo tubes, four in the bow and one astern, for which she carried eleven to fourteen torpedoes of two types: conventional and electrically driven. Submarines had mostly the electrically driven type, which gave off no bubbles on the surface. They did have a fault which was unknown in the early days. They had a nasty habit of not obeying the depth setting, and steered deeper than they should, passing under the keel of the target. Schuhart records that he missed at least five ships in 1940, and in the Norwegian campaign many English ships owed their continued existence to this fault.

Torpedoes also had two types of detonators: impact and magnetic. The latter had not been subjected to sufficient testing before being put into service, and often detonated before the bow after launching or before hitting the target. Schuhart was the first to experience this fault, which was later to have far-reaching effects.

U29 belonged to the Second Flotilla (Salzwedel) Wilhelmshaven, and began her life with training service (working up) in the North Sea and Baltic. She made two trips to Spain during the Spanish Civil War, but both of these were without incident.

In July 1939 the flotilla were training in the Baltic. On 21st July Admiral Raeder visited the Second and Seventh Flotilla, type Seven boats, and spoke to the captains, telling them that there would be no war because of Danzig.

In August, the Second Flotilla was on leave and Schuhart was in Austria. Dönitz was in Bad Gastein, also Austria, but that was not to be for long. On 16th August he received orders to report back to Wilhelmshaven, and on the 17th and 18th he was taking aboard equipment for war. On the 18th, Dönitz came to Wilhelmshaven to inform the captains of the political situation and to give them orders for the Atlantic operations. On 19th August they put to sea.

As U29 left Wilhelmshaven, there were no fanfares, no military bands, and no garlands of flowers bedecked the captain as they would later, on her return. Her orders were to sail unseen, proceed to the operational area, and wait.

As they left the Jade, Kapitanleutnant Otto Schuhart, as ordered, informed his crew of their destination and the political situation, and set his course north to pass through the North Sea.

They were not alone. Other boats had left Kiel with the same orders: sail unseen. War had not yet been declared; indeed, it was the belief of most of them that it would not come and that Hitler would even now manage to avert it, perhaps even manage to bring about another Munich. But this belief was tempered by their determination to be ready if it did.

Schuhart used every minute of the passage time training the crew, remaining submerged most of the time during the day, and carrying out exercises in deep steering and trimming drill, checking every seam, flange and gland in the boat. Every man knew that when the time came, he would have to function almost without thinking, and that any lapse of discipline, or inattention to orders or details would result in disaster.

The weather was good, with clear visibility and calm sea, the only difficulty being to avoid the traffic: the merchant shipping, and fishing vessels which abounded, particularly off the Norwegian coast. Two aircraft were sighted, and twice they sighted other boats of their flotilla, but had no contact with them.

On 24th August, in the late evening, they rounded the Faeroes, changed course to south-west, into the Atlantic, reaching their operational area, 50'N, 45'W, on 1st September.

Unlike Britain, Germany was ready, trained, poised, and ready to strike. They did not have long to wait for the fateful hour. At 1400 hours on 3rd September, Schuhart received the message: "Commence hostilities against British and French ships".

The feelings engendered by the order amongst the crew must have been myriad. Shock? Perhaps. Surprise? Very possibly. Disbelief? Amongst some, maybe. But fear and apprehension almost certainly not. Their high degree of training and readiness would have engendered a confidence which left little room for that.

On the 4th, the weather was not so good, but some ships were sighted. Some were neutral, and were therefore left alone in accordance with their orders to operate strictly in accordance with Prize Law. In some cases, the vessels sighted were travelling too quickly for U29.

On the 8th, U29 was blooded. The tanker *Regent Tiger* was sighted and stopped by gunfire. The crew were ordered to leave the ship, and she was sunk by torpedoes.

Four days later, on the 12th, Schuhart stopped the High Sea Tug *Neptunia* and decided to sink her by torpedo, using the new magnetic type. What followed was to have far-reaching effects for both the U-boat Arm and their prey.

The first torpedo detonated before the bow of U29, and the second, before the *Neptunia*. Schuhart knew immediately that something was wrong, and ordered the loading of the old impact torpedoes, which did their deadly work.

Schuhart was the first to experience the failure of the new magnetic torpedo, and immediately passed on his discovery to the other boats in the flotilla. Had he not decided to test the new weapon at this early stage, then this story at least, would very possibly not have been written, and the lives of 518 British seamen would probably not have been lost five days later. Also, U29 would probably have become the victim of escorting destroyers, as did U39 which had been sunk only three days previously on the 14th after Schuhart had warned her commander about the faulty magnetic torpedoes.

On the 14th, another tanker, the *British Influence*, fell prey to U29. Again, this happened after her crew had been evacuated and were picked up by a neutral ship.

The curtain had been raised on the longest and bloodiest battle of the war, a war of attrition which was to bleed the protagonists white before it ended six years later; a war which started in actuality on 19th August 1939, when Schuhart and seventeen of his companions sailed to take up their positions, which had been decided some time before, and ended only after the official armistice when all the U-boats had been given instructions as to how to surrender, and it was feared that some might decide to fight on, or at least attempt some last grand gesture. In fact 154 surrendered after the armistice, but 218 were scuttled by their crews when it was realised that the end was inevitable.

Germany started the war with fifty-seven U-boats, and when the war ended, a total of 1153 had been built. Germany claimed over 3,500 ships sunk, totalling 18.3 million tons. But British records give a figure of 2,603 ships, totalling 12.8 million tons sunk in the Atlantic.

There can be no doubt that the U-boat Arm took a massive toll in the Battle of Atlantic. At one time in the early days they were sinking ships faster than we could build them. That was in what the U-boat fraternity called the 'happy times'. But before long, the tide turned. The night of 8th March 1941 saw the destruction of U47, Günther Prien's boat, and U100 commanded by Joachim Schepke a few hours later. Within a week U99 was depth charged and forced to surface, and Otto Kretschmer and his crew were captured. Thus Dönitz lost his three top aces within a week, and from then on U-boat losses mounted - until by the end of hostilities, of the 40,000 officers and men in the U-boat Arm, over 26,000 were dead. By any standard, a bloodletting on both sides unparalleled in the history of war.

Chapter Four

The Protagonists: Captain William Tofield Makeig-Jones RN

William Tofield Makeig-Jones was a big man. A big man in every way. Physically, he towered above most other men, and exuded an impression of solidity and reliability. He was very representative of the Navy at that time, and from those that served both with him and under him, a picture emerged of a breed of man that seemed to spring so frequently from a mould which the Navy was fortunate enough to possess during those years between the wars.

Born in 1890 at Wath upon Dearne, Yorkshire, he was educated at St Paul's School and the RN College HMS *Britannia* at Dartmouth. In 1910, he was a lieutenant specialising in Torpedoes and Communications, (Wireless Telegraphy). From 1914-1918 he was wireless officer on the staff of the Admiral who at that time was second in command of the Grand Fleet, and served in the battleship HMS *Marlborough*, sistership of *Benbow* and *Iron Duke*, at Jutland. It was during this period that he became heavyweight boxing champion of the Royal Navy. He also played rugby for the Navy.

He was promoted to lieutenant commander in 1921 and in the same year married Dorothy Faulkner at Torquay. Promotion to commander came two years later in 1923, and he was appointed to the aircraft-carrier *Furious* as executive officer. It was here that he gained the experience that no doubt resulted in his being appointed to *Courageous*. He later became signals officer to the Dept of Admiralty, and qualified at Staff College.

The year 1930 saw his promotion to captain, whilst serving as executive officer in HMS *Royal Oak* in the Mediterranean, and shortly after he commanded the destroyer HMS *Valentine* as second in command of the Second Destroyer Flotilla.

From 1933–35 he commanded the cruisers HMS *Cardiff* and *Dorsetshire* as flag captain to Admiral Sir Edward Evans on the Africa Station, His Royal Highness Prince George, later Duke of York, being one of his lieutenants. Following this, he was appointed to the Admiralty as director of the Signals Dept.

It was very obvious that Capt. Makeig-Jones was destined for Flag rank when in 1937 he was appointed to flag captain in HMS *Nelson*, the flagship of the home fleet. This was considered a plum appointment in the service. In July 1939 he was appointed commodore at Portsmouth Barracks, and was to have taken up the appointment in the October. But here fate took a hand, and in August, while he was on six weeks' leave, the longest period he had ever had, he was given command of HMS *Courageous*, which had just completed repairs and a refit and had been recommissioned on 31st July. She was to be his last command.

The son of a doctor, who had moved his family to Torquay in the early 1900s and had returned to Seaton, Devon, William Makeig-Jones settled into a cottage in nearby Beer. There was one son of his marriage, who was educated at Wellington, and later, while serving in the Fleet Air Arm, was awarded a DSC in the air fighting over Norway. He left the Navy after the war, and was tragically murdered in Ceylon while managing a tea estate.

The captain was one of three brothers and three sisters, the eldest of whom Susanna (or Daisy) was the famous designer of the Wedgwood Fairyland lustreware. His name is on the Seaton Devon War Memorial.

There can be little doubt that William Makeig-Jones was destined to attain high rank in the service. His rapid rise to the rank of captain, and appointment to command HMS *Nelson* as flag captain of the home fleet flagship, and later, his appointment as commodore at Portsmouth, which is the last step towards flag rank, put the seal on a career which was only interrupted when he was appointed to command *Courageous*, at a time when the service so desperately needed captains with experience of aircraft-carriers.

He was also a personal friend of Captain Lord Louis Mountbatten, whose speciality, Communications and Wireless, he shared. Captain Makeig-Jones cannot be better described than by the words of one of the survivors of *Courageous*, Ronald Bell, who, as a young signalman at that time, wrote "I remember our captain, Makeig-Jones, a great sailor and gentleman, sitting on his bridge stool, puffing his pipe, with his cap slightly tilted, and his fine fresh West Country face looking pink and bluff. Occasionally, it fell to my lot to take signals to him in his cabin. He always smiled, and said, 'Thank you'. He really was a fine man."

I was told by his nephew that he had once said, "If I ever lose my ship, I will go with her." Like all others of his kind, he kept faith. Yes, he really was a fine man. One which Britain could ill afford to lose.

Chapter Five

Kapitanleutnant Otto Schuhart

Otto Schuhart was born in Hamburg on 1st April 1909. The son of a merchant, he spent his early life in Magdeburg and Hamburg, his family having little connection with the sea. He graduated from high school in Hamburg in the autumn of 1928. In 1929, he became a naval officer candidate in the Reichmarine, and was commissioned as a sub-lieutenant in October 1922, and appointed to the line ship *Schleswig-Holstein*. Later appointments were to the Third Dept Marine Artillery at Schwinemunde; as group officer, adjutant. Submarine flotilla *Weddingen*; flag lieutenant; commander training.

He commanded submarines U8, U25, joining U29 in April 1939.

He carried out war patrols in the North Atlantic and the approaches to Britain from 19th August 1939 (just prior to the outbreak of war) until January 1941. The results of these patrols were the destruction of 60,000 tons of shipping, and the aircraft-carrier *Courageous*.

He then became company commander of the first Submarine Division, training commanders and watch officers, and at the same time commander of the Twenty-first Submarine flotilla at the training centre at Pillau. He was then appointed commander 1st Division at the naval academy at Flensburg-Murwik, officer candidate training.

At the end of the war, after closing down the Academy, he was a prisoner of war until dismissed from the Navy in December 1945, when it was disbanded.

His family's last residence was at Pillau, and after the occupation of that city, and the loss of all their belongings, they found refuge at Satrup, near Flensburg.

Otto Schuhart embarked upon civilian life as an unskilled worker at a local company, and later moved to Hamburg, where the Stulcken Shipyard, which was under reconstruction, offered him the management of the apprentices department, and the duties of shipyard captain. His real aim, however, was re-entry into his former naval career. This came about in December 1955, when he joined the Navy of the Federal Republic of Germany.

His first appointment was as group officer in charge of the testing and selection of navy officer candidates. This was followed by appointment as vice commander of the Naval Academy at Murwik, after its re-establishment, responsible for training activities. He became official training advisor to the Navy staff, followed by commander of the naval base at Kiel, and then commander of the Navy training regiment. He retired in September 1967 with the rank of Kapitan Zur See (Captain). His decorations were:

Iron Cross 1st and 2nd Class.
Knight's Cross of the Iron Cross
War Merits Cross with Swords 1st and 2nd Class
Federal Merits Cross 1st and 2nd Class
Submarine Combat Medal

This was the CV given to me personally by Kapt. Schuhart and bears his signature.

I was in correspondence with Kapt. Schuhart from the end of October 1982, until his death in March 1990, and indeed, apart from British Intelligence, was the only one to ask him detailed questions regarding the sinking of the *Courageous*. We corresponded for eight years, and during the whole period he went to great pains to answer all my very numerous questions very fully and frankly, which at times must have been very trying for him, owing to my very poor knowledge of the German language.

From his account, there emerges a story of a chain of coincidences and happenings, which strangely build up into a scenario which could only have one culmination. If this story had been a novel, it would not have taken the reader long to realise that a dreadful disaster was pending. It would very quickly become clear that the point of no return came very close to the beginning. From that point, the sky darkens with the clouds of foreboding. From the beginning of our acquaintance, there seemed to grow an understanding which, over the period of eight years of correspondence, grew into a mutual respect, which when we met seemed to have the tacit agreement of us both. But this is something that it is best to explain later.

Chapter Six

Girding of Loins

In the year between the Munich crisis and the outbreak of hostilities it is questionable how much was done to make up the leeway in preparing *Courageous* for action. It was obvious to all but the blind that there were glaring gaps. *Courageous* herself had only been recommissioned at the end of July after a refit, the extent of which seems difficult to gauge. The available extracts from the Board of Inquiry on 21st September 1939 show that criticism was made of the fact that the ring main was not split, which virtually meant that if severed, as it was, there would be no power throughout the ship. This, as will be seen later, resulted in heavy loss of life. Although many reservists had been mobilised in 1938, it would appear that not much had been learned from the exercise, as some men were joining the ship with civilian clothes and moustaches, having been so hastily called back from the reserve list.

The heavy loss of life was added to by the fact that *Courageous* had more than her reasonable share of recalled pensioners; men who, in a life-threatening situation, stood a very reduced likelihood of survival in the water. There was also the fact that there was no general issue of life jackets, and that many of the Carley floats could not be released from the stowage brackets as these had been continually painted over in situ. Also there were reported cases of ladders not being secured to hatch coamings.

All the ship's boats and motorboats and launches, with the exception of the whaler, which had rope falls, were operated electrically, and this resulted in a great loss of life, particularly in the case of non-swimmers and pensioners.

Courageous herself was, for a ship of her age and size, perfectly seaworthy, but it could not be expected that, in the very short space of time the ship's company had to shake down, all the training and exercises could have been carried out, particularly bearing in mind that many were recalled pensioners who had been away from the service for anything up to ten years, and in the case of men who had left the service after twelve years, their training would have almost been forgotten. Also there were young reservists from all walks of life who had never been to sea. Add to that the fact that the ship was immediately sent out on anti-submarine patrols and the crew were learning their jobs as they went along, then things like damage control and personnel safety could not have played a very big part in their training at sea at that stage of the war.

There can be no doubt whatsoever that the sending out of *Courageous*, *Hermes* and *Ark Royal* on anti-submarine patrols was a hastily cobbled-together measure which would never have been attempted had there been any feasible alternative that stood any real chance of success. To begin with, an aircraft-carrier is about the biggest target you can imagine at sea and needs to keep moving fast to have any chance of survival, and then needs at least four escorts for herself alone. *Ark Royal* had an escort of six destroyers, possibly because she was our best and newest carrier. *Courageous* and *Hermes* had only four, and if a submarine contact or report was made then two of these would have to be detached, as in the case when *Courageous* sent a striking force off to help the steamer *Kaferistan*. She was left in one of the most vulnerable situations imaginable. Indeed, after the near miss experienced by *Ark Royal* on 14th September, one can hardly believe the other two were not recalled immediately. It was admitted that the Carrier anti-submarine hunting groups were hastily put together pending the setting up of the convoy system, which proves that lessons were not learned from the previous war when the convoy system was most successful.

To sum up, *Courageous* herself, despite her age, was not an unsound ship. She had one very great advantage: that of being a very fast ship. But a carrier by her very nature is very cumbersome; also, the design dictates a certain amount of loss of watertight integrity by virtue of the fact that the large areas of the hangar space and lifts allow large volumes of water to swill around once it comes aboard, thus adding to any slight list taken on by holing below the water line; also the movement of aircraft and gear caused by listing would add to the already serious possibility of her capsizing. Another factor in the case of *Courageous* was that as she was moving at a fairly high speed when the torpedoes struck, her forward motion would have greatly increased the inflow of water and therefore the degree of list. This in turn made it impossible to use any boats which might have been lowered by means other than from electrical power.

Chapter Seven
The Last Patrol

We were ill-prepared from the start. It was as if we thought that if we tried to convince ourselves that it would not happen, then it wouldn't. But all the time, we knew that it would come to it eventually. Dictators never alter, and their appetites are never satisfied, and grow with feeding.

When *Courageous* sailed on her last voyage, men were joining the ship up to the last minute; a few of them had never actually been to sea before, having had only very basic training. Many of the recalled pensioners had been away from the service for some years, and some were over fifty years of age, which in terms of warship service is considered an old man.

It takes time for a ship's company to 'shake down'. First they have to get to know each other and their officers. Then they gradually get back into a routine that they have been away from for some time, and get used to doing their old jobs again. This has next to build up into a state of efficiency through drills and exercises which engender confidence in themselves and their shipmates, and finally becomes honed into an efficient machine, in which each man performs confidently.

Courageous was commissioned on 31st July after a refit, and there had been no time to achieve this between then and the six weeks before her sinking. All the ship's company had to learn a completely new role in order to take her to sea hunting U-boats. This had never been done with carriers before, and to ask this of a hastily brought together crew, many with little or no experience, and a number of RAF personnel who actually kept the aircraft flying, and to expect that they would know anything of 'Damage Control' and the niceties of shipboard life is asking a great deal. But when it became important, they acquitted themselves very well in the circumstances. Such is war, and there was no option. Through a series of mistakes and stupidity perpetrated by politicians and complacent civil servants, aided and abetted by some service chiefs who were more interested in enlarging their own sphere of influence than the long-term good of the service and country, we were unprepared. The Anti-Submarine division of the naval staff established in World War I had been abolished as a post-war economy, and was only re-established in the autumn of 1939 - very late in the day in view of the success of the U-boats in the first war.

While it is difficult to obtain accurate information on naval policy and thinking in the years just prior to the war, it is not being too unfair to arrive at certain conclusions. The First World War showed what tremendous damage could be done by the U-boat, which then so very nearly turned the tide in Germany's favour. One can only wonder why, when it became obvious that we were slowly drifting with increasing momentum towards another war, we didn't take the necessary steps soon enough and get our anti-submarine act together. At that time the range of aircraft was limited, and land-based aircraft could only search for U-boats and escort convoys for a very short distance from their bases before having to return. This of course meant that the U-boat's greatest enemy, the aircraft, could only operate from a carrier, and we just did not have enough.

This was the reason for the three hunter groups formed. *Ark Royal* with an escort of six destroyers, and *Courageous* and *Hermes* each with an escort of four. But they would not have been necessary if we had had small carriers, such as the attacker class: escort carriers which were, compared with fleet carriers, inexpensive, unsophisticated fly-on fly-off carriers, and which proved themselves invaluable from the moment they came into service. But sending three fleet carriers with such scanty protection to look for U-boats was, as one survivor put it, "Like sending a young virgin out into a street full of rapists". After one disaster, and a near miss in two weeks, we gave it up.

Extracts from the Board of Inquiry 21.9.39

No written orders were issued for AS3. The third anti-submarine patrol of *Courageous*.

The operation for which *Courageous* left Plymouth at 11.39 on 16th September 1939 was to follow the pattern of two previous operations of the same nature; the second being on 9th September 1939, with *Kempenfelt*, *Ardent* and *Echo* as escort.

Captain Makeig-Jones was at the Area Combined Headquarters on Tuesday 14th, and the intended operation was discussed then. The commanding officer of *Hermes*, which was engaged in similar A/S operations was also present. The Admiralty appreciation of the operation was brought to the commander-in-chief by Commander Peder of the Naval Air Division, and was discussed with both commanding officers, and they were each given a copy of the appreciation, also of an Admiralty memorandum of June 1938 entitled "Anti-submarine Striking Forces". It was made clear to both COs that they were not tied in any way by the appreciation. They were given a free hand as regards the conduct of their operations, subject to the limitations given in the C-in-C's Western Approaches 1917/15th and 1951/16th.

The object was given as the destruction of enemy submarines, and it was impressed on the CO of *Courageous* that once contact had been made with a submarine, it should be hunted until it was destroyed.

The date and time of the *Courageous*' sailing was not decided until Captain (D)3, and the Fifth Division had arrived, as they were required to act as *Courageous*' escort and striking force. The proposed operation was discussed with Captain (D)3 on Friday 15th September, but the commanding officer of *Courageous* was not present. Captain (D)3, however, visited him before sailing on Saturday 16th to discuss the operation.

Commander Dan Baker, the senior observer of *Courageous*, visited Area Combined Headquarters p.m. on Friday 15th September, to obtain the latest information as to our disposition and enemy submarines.

On the evening of Friday 15th September, all the ship's company of *Courageous* were recalled from shore leave. This must have taken some organisation. Notices were displayed in cinemas, and naval patrols visited all the public houses in Devonport and Plymouth, and all the other places of amusement in the two towns. It would also have meant the police and patrols calling at the addresses of all the ship's company who lived locally. When *Courageous* sailed, not one officer or rating was missing. This was a fantastic achievement in a blacked-out city with very little transport. In those days very few private homes had telephones; certainly not those supported by a sailor's pay.

Courageous left Plymouth at 10.30 on Saturday 16th September with an escort of four escorting destroyers, *Inglefield* Capt(D) *Intrepid*, *Ivanhoe* and *Impulsive*, and proceeded into the Atlantic to carry out offensive air operations against enemy submarines.

HMS *Hermes*, with four "I" class destroyers of the Third Flotilla was already at sea, and the instructions were that *Courageous* should operate to the northward of a line drawn 250° from Land's End, and *Hermes* to the southward of it. Subsequent to leaving harbour, both aircraft-carriers were ordered in addition to operate to the westward of longitude 12° W, as shore-based aircraft would search to the eastward of this line. The destroyers were formed in anti submarine screen No 3, i.e. one ahead, one astern, and one on either beam, at a distance of half a mile, and during daylight hours, an anti-submarine air patrol of three aircraft, searching at a distance of fifteen miles on either side of the ship.

Chapter Eight

Extract from the Log of the U29

Between 1605hrs 17th Sept. and 2100hrs 19th Sept. 1939
Kommandant: Kapitanleutnant Schuhart

Date and time	*Description of position, sea state, wind, weather, light, visibility, moon, etc.*	
17.9	East 2, Sea state 2-3, long swell, clear, sunny, very good vis	In waiting position on the American steamer route.
1605	.	Steamer approaching from the west. Seen late because he comes directly out of the sun. The boat is apparently on his general track. Course 080, speed 13–14 knots.
1617		Submerged. Steamer zigzags, English. Freighter with passenger-carrying capability. What is it being used for? Size about 10,000 tons, Manchester Line? Steamer does not zigzag long, therefore the passing distance will be quite large, about 5,000m. Now I see that he is flying a reddish flag and I am getting suspicious about the nationality, perhaps American? - Suddenly I see an aircraft approaching from astern at low altitude next to the steamer - war materials then, or troop transport. Decision to fire a torpedo. Steamer zigzags away before torpedo can be fired. Angle is getting too wide. Intention: After it is out of sight to surface, keep in contact, and carry out a surprise attack at night. At the same time prepare for R/T. Report for the boats further east. Course 080 - because of the air cover down to 20m.

1800 At 13m look around. Ahead to port a square-shaped cloud on the horizon: not a smoke cloud but an aircraft-carrier, assumed to be *Ark Royal*. Range more than 10,000m, course south west. I can recognise the masts of an escort destroyer ahead of the aircraft-carrier. I realise immediately that the aircraft observed by the steamer belongs not to him but to *Ark Royal*. Moving U29 at slow speed toward the ships. I estimate half ahead. I can't see the air cover; I'm looking for more escorts in the distance, without success. As to the close escort I find the destroyer ahead, one astern and one on each side. The boats ahead and astern are stationed about 1,000m from the carrier, I can't form a clear picture about the ones on his beam.

1845 The carrier turns onto 270, westerly heading; I go to 360. Decision: to fire three (Etos?) as a fan with a narrow spread in order to achieve possibly two hits. Depth setting 6m. The reason I don't trust magnetic torpedoes is because of the experience with *Neptunia*. Concerning the convoy I can see two aircraft occasionally circling over the two other ships.

1900 The range on the beam is too high (about 7,000m). By varying the heading I suddenly realise the speed is rather high (20 knots). I am running at periscope depth constantly watching the carrier zigzagging. Having seen the zigzagging of the British, I do not yet need to give up the hope of getting him. The carrier had increased his range from me when he suddenly turned at least 70° on to a southerly heading (225); medium speed. Later on he turns onto 180. From now on everything develops quickly. Calculations started for angle on the bow 90 and speed 15, I estimate that the passing distance for angle on the bow 90 will be 3,000m, but I am also ready to fire at a greater range; I can expect the Etos to run for 4-5,000m. I have nothing to use as a reference for distance because of the enormous height of freeboard of the carrier, plus I have to look into the sun. For the same reason it is difficult to estimate my relative position. The periscope is from time to time just beneath the surface as I am running at right angles to the swell. Because of the risk of detection speed slow or dead slow. Attack depth 14m, attack heading 240.

1950 lat 50° 5'N long 14° 20'W — In the turn hard starboard, three torpedoes fired; angle on the bow 100. Aiming points about 20m ahead of the bow, amidships and 20m astern. On firing I see the port side destroyer 500m ahead of the boat. Hard starboard to 360, both engines full ahead and quickly down to 50m. The boat climbed very little after the launch of the three torpedoes and the Chief Engineer has all well in hand.

1953 — In the whole boat we can clearly hear the explosions from two torpedo hits, timed running time was 2 mins 15 secs, equivalent to 2,100m; immediately after the second hit an enormous detonation followed by a few smaller ones. The noise is so loud that I have the impression that we ourselves have been damaged. - Jubilation in the boat, although everyone is apprehensive about what will happen next. The behaviour of the carrier between 1900 and 1922 is unclear to me. It is possible that a change in the air situation took place and he had to decrease speed rapidly. I saw nothing to explain that. The boat is meanwhile down to 60m and because we apparently have no ill effects from this depth we can go down to 80m. Because of water in the boat (stern gland etc.), the limited use of engines and because of the danger of detection, not being able to use the pumps, the boat gets so heavy that we go further down to 105m. The boat is behaving magnificently.

From 100m on we can hear a tinkling noise on the upper deck - considered to be a search sonar but it has to be caused by the pressure at this depth. During the entire chase we remained at 80m, both engines slow ahead and when necessary dead slow.

1959 Loud propeller noises quickly approaching the boat and passing overhead. Four depth charges falling – exploding directly overhead but far too high (60m). Strong vibrations in the boat. I am standing in the conning tower which shakes completely. No apparent changes in depth. A few minutes later another six depth charges with the same result. The third time they drop a little further away, but this time the vibrations do not appear. The concert of depth charges around the boat, appearing and disappearing, last until 2200 – the distance increases steadily.

At 2200 the boat is approximately 4nm away from the attack position, however by midnight we are reasonably certain that we have escaped detection.

The following details were observed:

	Ship's Bearing	*Range*	*Depth*	
1950	–	2500m	14m	Three torpedoes fired.
1952	170	2500m	–	Carrier's propeller noise.
1953	–	ditto	40m	One torpedo hit followed by detonation much stronger than the first with more following.
1959	155–330	600m	60m	Destroyer propeller noise – starboard astern to starboard ahead. Boat passed over by two destroyers. Four loud depth charge detonations overhead from astern to ahead. Simultaneously weaker detonations on each side – destroyers obviously running in line abreast.
2001	–	increasing	80m	Destroyers moving away. Continuous detonations in close proximity to the boat and then further away.
2003	280	decreasing	90–100m	Two destroyers coming nearer – one running over the boat between conning tower and bow – six loud detonations – destroyers apparently again in line abreast.
2004	not measurable	constant	80-100m	Everywhere in the boat tapping noises in the rhythm of a sonar transmitter. In our receiver loud tinkling noises like boiling water.
2008	–	not measured.		Destroyers coming closer –
2020			80-100m	Detonations in close proximity to the boat and some on top but much shallower setting.

2020 2041	–	not measured	80–100m	Destroyers have stopped and are launching depth charges in a larger radius.
2041 2156	–	200-6000m	80-100m	Destroyers apparently forming search formation. Numerous explosions – it sounds as if they are dropping 40-50 depth charges in one position – each time further away from the boat.
2156 2321	–	–	80m	Propeller noises moving astern – recording bearing from time to time 291–075.
2321 2340	250	4000m	80m	Propeller noises getting stronger and moving astern. Boat turns 10 degrees to starboard – noise moving to 140 and getting quieter – only a few detonations.
2356	–	–	60m	Propeller noises getting weaker and no longer measurable.
0135				Surfaced.

Comprehensively speaking one has to say that the torpedo launching position was immediately detected by the destroyers, but the three times that they passed over the boat does not confirm that they had sonar contact but that they only used a search pattern without intercept datums. Echo impulses like our 'S' equipment were not detected. The tapping on the boat is unexplained, apparently only search transmissions. Throughout the chase my own speed was either slow or dead slow with both engines. My own receiver capability at great depth was very good and without noise disturbance. The observations from Obergefreiter Schroter on the G.H.G. were made with exceptional calm and composure also during the critical phases. Questions concerning the boat: During the entire time under water the Chief Engineer, Oberleutnant (Eng) Laufs kept the boat completely under control and his quietness and superiority were quickly appreciated not only by the control team but by the whole crew. All in all the attitude of the crew was good. They had all, through books and magazines, a mental picture of what it might be like but the reality was worse than they had imagined. The crew were worn out by the extended chase and recovered slowly throughout the next day.

		The destroyer was able to detect my firing position as he was able to see both torpedoes hit the port side of the carrier and must have recognised the pressure outrush of the three torpedoes. The first depth charges were dropped in this position. Together with the destroyer positioned astern he then started the chase. But apart from the first depth charge pattern he was never able to spot the correct position of the boat. A second possibility as to how he started on the right track may be that the torpedoes passing under the destroyer were seen. The red warheads must have been seen up to ten metres deep in the clear Atlantic water.
18.9 0100	East 2 Sea state 2 clear, bright night, sunny by day good visibility	Propeller noise has disappeared astern. Nothing important has been heard for an hour. The boat is moving slowly up to 23m. Heard a sharp crack which must have been caused by the expansion of the plates.
0135		Hatch open. Course 340 speed 13 knots. Intention: to move as far away as possible from the attack position until dawn and then investigate the state of the boat. The result is that the boat is completely intact apart from the attack periscope. No traces of depth charges or pressure effects on the upper deck. The attack periscope is full of water, which has got in through the neck. After 24 hours of drying out all mirrors are covered in grease and dirt. The attack periscope is U/S. The question is: how successful was U29's attack? I cannot decide to return and attack again should the ship have been only badly damaged as I have run low on attack weapons, attack periscope U/S, only one G7a and one Eto in the bow tubes and fuel enough only for a direct course back to base. The conviction is that the ship was destroyed. The explosions were so loud that the ship either must have disintegrated or exploded.
1000		Returning to base. At 1200 I received information from British radio confirming the success of

		U29. We did not sink *Ark Royal* but *Courageous* and they say that we were also destroyed. Tremendous pleasure in the boat. Passage speed 10 knts. At night in calm water and luminosity of the water is such that the boat, despite the slow speed, must be visible for miles. It appears as if the boat's waterline is illuminated with small lamps. One is able to see shoals of fish near the boat during the periods when the water is lit up.
19.9	Calm, no swell, good to medium visibility.	R/T report made reference RTB and the destruction of the *Courageous*. No traffic observed on the western steamer route leading to the Irish Sea. Reception of the appreciation of the C-in-C and the award of the Iron Cross to the crew.
20.9	WSW 2 Sea state 1 clear, sunny, good visibility.	
1300		I decide to shorten the route by crossing between the Shetlands and Faeroes. The lookout is now so capable that even if they are monitoring the straits we do not fear detection provided that the visibility remains good. - Nothing seen.
21.9	WSW 2 Sea state 3 Swell from west rapid decrease in temperature - a.m. fog - p.m. moderate vis.	Trusting the good visibility the boat passed very close to the Faeroes in order to stay well clear of the English reconnaissance bases thought to be in the Orkneys. In the forenoon the boat ran into some fishing boats in the mist and dived.

Chapter Nine

Abandon Ship

From here on, the stories of the men and their relatives take over. They are many and varied, and some may appear to contradict others, as in all such stories. Not because anyone is spinning a yarn or making things up, but because in such dire circumstances as these, each man is often in a little world sometimes only measuring a few feet, and in fear of his life, and cannot bring his mind to focus on anything outside this tiny area of immediate danger until he begins to come to terms gradually with the situation.

The two marked instances of this are when one survivor stated that his worst problem while in the water was oil fuel; not just a small amount, but masses of it, which gummed up his eyes to such an extent that he was almost blinded by it, and afraid that he would swim in the wrong direction and perhaps be sucked under when this massive ship went down; or go so far away from her that the ships attempting to pick them up would not see him, covered with oil as he was. Another man when asked about the problem of oil in the water replied, "Rubbish, I didn't see any oil fuel at all, and neither did anyone near me". The reason was that the fuel tanks on the port side were ruptured when the two torpedoes struck, and the immediate list to port resulted in large quantities of oil escaping from the tanks.

Another instance of conflicting stories occurs when we read that several officers saw a periscope fine on the port quarter, showing up against the reflected glow in the water from the western sky. They loaded a 4.7" gun on the starboard side, but because of the heavy list to port could not train it. Also several officers and ratings stated that they saw the end of a submarine come out of the water after a depth charge attack by *Ivanhoe*. But the script of Schuhart's report clearly shows that this was not so. In situations such as this, it is so easy to make mistakes, errors, or see things that are not really there. Only those who have been in a truly life-threatening situation can begin to realise how much the world can shrink in such a short time, and the mind concentrates within that world, as it must if the body is to survive. Truly, the onlooker sees most of the game, but it is easy to understand that the participants in this situation pay the ultimate penalty if they fail to concentrate in this particular game.

Immediately after the explosion of the two torpedoes, the quartermaster at the wheel reported that the ship would not steer. The captain ordered that the ship's position be given to the W/T office, and that the signal books be collected on the signal bridge and the unweighted ones be put in canvas bags and taken to the compass platform ready for destruction.

About ten minutes after the ship was struck, some bulkheads were heard to collapse, and the immediate 20° list that the ship had taken on increased to 35°. At the same time the captain ordered the international signal "Stand by me" to be hoisted. This was done. He then said that anyone who wished to leave the ship was at liberty to do so.

In the engine room department Lt. (E) Shenton, who was on watch in the forward centre engine room, ordered the engines to be stopped. He then ordered the evacuation of the engine room. It can only be imagined how difficult it was to carry out the standard duties needed in such an emergency in such awesome conditions. Apart from battery lighting, there was no power at all, and the increasing list to port would have made even moving about a very hazardous task. The steam pressure was falling rapidly, and there was a considerable leak in the port side, caused by the torpedo damage. He operated the emergency bulkhead valve closing lever, and rang the sprayer telegraph to zero. As he was leaving the engine room the revolution telegraph from the bridge was rung down.

A stoker coming up from the boiler room with his overalls on fire could give no information on the situation; others coming up later could not give any statements; frankly, it is not surprising that in such a situation men were not able to make very accurate comment re the conditions in the engine room. Once the order to abandon is given by an officer, the recipient is only too ready to obey.

Meanwhile, between decks, very little action could be taken. All important watertight doors were already closed, and the remainder could not be closed. The captain gave the order to flood the starboard bilges, but although the order did not get through Lt. (E) Sedgewick, and a stoker PO from the double bottom party, with the help of a sub-lieutenant (A), carrying a torch, proceeded to Z seacock to attempt to flood the starboard bilges. They succeeded in removing the cotter pin, but in spite of a wheel spanner being used, the valve could not be turned.

On the starboard side of the upper deck, all attempts to launch boats failed, as they were turned in and secured, and required electrical power to release them. The only exception was a seaboat (cutter) which had rope falls, but when attempts were made to lower it, they were unsuccessful because of the tremendous list to port, and the boat overturned against the ship's side, spilling the occupants into the sea.

Action taken on the upper deck with regard to boats was limited because of the already steep list to port, at this time 20°–30°. On the port side, the fourth motor launch right aft was traversed out, and some ratings were able to unhook the falls as soon as it was waterborne. Owing to the list of the ship it was only possible to cast loose about three Carley floats on the starboard side, but some loose woodwork and gratings were thrown over the side.

There were reports of some people in the water being struck by objects coming over the side and many injuries due to men leaving the ship and sustaining quite severe damage in uncontrolled falls on to the bulges, and serious abrasions and worse caused by men sliding down the barnacle encrusted bulges, including one man whose buttocks were very badly lacerated in one such slide, and another very nearly emasculated sliding down the bulges facing them.

In the aircraft hangars there was considerable confusion caused by aircraft breaking loose, and other gear sliding about, again owing to the heavy and increasing list, and in the lower hangar, men had difficulty in forcing their way through the fire curtains which were jammed down after the explosion, again owing to the total loss of power throughout the ship.

The key of the cypher chest was taken over by Paymaster Lt. Evans shortly after the torpedoes struck, but the paymaster commander ordered him not to ditch the chest over the side for the moment. But later, when it became obvious that the ship was sinking, the steel chest was found to have slid away from its stowage, and there could be no doubt that it sank with the ship.

Immediately after the torpedoes hit, *Ivanhoe* on the port bow attacked the submarine, and two patterns of depth charges were dropped. *Impulsive* on the starboard side was ordered by *Ivanhoe* to stand by the stricken carrier and dropped astern to begin picking up survivors.

Schuhart reported in his log that four depth charges had exploded directly overhead, but far too high (60m) yet there were strong vibrations in the boat. He was standing in the conning tower, which he said was shaking, and a few minutes later another six depth charges exploded with the same result. The third time, he said that they dropped a little further away, "But this time vibrations do not affect the boat." He goes on to say, "The concert of depth charges around the boat, appearing and disappearing, lasted until 2200 hours – the distance increased steadily."

Chapter Ten

Over the Side

At the time of the sinking Lt.-Cdr. Criddle was a young leading torpedo man and duty electrician. The torpedo branch looked after all the ship's electrics. He had the first dog watch, and had just nipped into the paravane store, which was the torpedo man's hideout for a smoke. "That smoke literally saved my life," he told me. "I'd no sooner closed the door when, bang! The first explosion was closely followed by the second. The brass bezel or ring around the glass porthole shot out. I wondered what the hell had happened, but it only took a second or two to realise that we had been tin-fished (torpedoed). Almost immediately the ship began to list, and instinctively I made for the starboard side, knowing that it was the side farthest away from the damage, and the highest point. It is funny how instinctive that sort of thing is, you never consciously thought about it.

"From what I heard later, I believe that the torpedoes struck, one, just above the bomb room, and the other adjacent to the main switchboard. There was no panic, but an almost eerie silence for a few moments while everyone got their wits together. Another reason for the silence was that the electrics right throughout the ship were knocked out at one stroke and there was no communication, except by shouted orders."

Only two cutters could be manually lowered. "The starboard cutter hit the bulge of the ship because of her increasing list to port and tipped its occupants into the sea." He laughed as he told me that when he started peeling off his clothes, he thought, "I'd better keep my socks and undershirt on to keep my feet warm and the bare necessities. Whatever made me think that I don't know. I still kept on my overalls and my pusser's belt with the little money pouch with five pound notes in it."

Life-saving equipment was almost non-existent; Carley floats were stuck in position by paint that had been applied year after year, and efforts to free them were useless. Watertight compartments were not watertight, due to continually being painted, and had not been checked for proper closure. Ladders were not secured over hatch coamings and consequently became unshipped due to the increasing list of the ship which was already down by the head. To add to the problem, many men were injured when damage control timbers were jettisoned over the side to provide men in the water with something to cling on to; exactly how many can only be guessed at.

"I left the ship by lowering myself down by a paravane wire. I forgot that the wires of a paravane were serrated for cutting the mooring wires of mines so that they would float to the surface. After lowering myself a few feet my hands began to smoke, so I let go and plunged the rest of the way into the water, getting away with only minor burns to my hands.

"I was a good swimmer and struck out for the *Impulsive*. She was about half a mile away. The water wasn't rough, and there were no breaks in the wave tops, but, there was a fairly heavy Atlantic swell, which didn't make swimming easy. To the contrary, each time the swell came you swam uphill for a bit, then free wheeled down the other side. I think the swell could have been the thing that beat most of the older men. I could see bodies floating motionless, and others who had just about given up. Asking men in their fifties to swim that sort of distance in a heavy swell is too much to expect.

"I remember a man called Pete Jackson swimming near me. He looked as if any minute he was going to give up, and the destroyer by this time was not far away. I was a bit rude to him, I shouted at him in a loud voice. I think I probably made him angry, because he seemed to liven up a bit. Anyway we got over to *Impulsive*, and I let him go first. He was an old man about fifty. When we got aboard he said to me, 'Thanks Jim'. 'What for?' I asked. 'Cussing at me,' he said. 'I was just about done for, and being cussed at like that was what I needed to get me going.'

"When we landed, and after survivor's leave, Pete went to torpedo school and I was sent to Barrow-in-Furness, which was Pete's home town, to join HMS *Illustrious*, a new carrier. He gave me a letter, and asked me if I would take it to his mother. When I got to Barrow, the ship was nearing completion but not ready to accommodate us, so we had to get digs ashore. Anyway, I called on Pete's mother and gave her his letter, in which he had obviously told her about the incident when I cussed at him. As soon as she knew that I had to find digs, she said, 'Right, you're not going any further than our front door, you'll stay here.' I had never had any contact with the North before, but the hospitality of those people is past belief.

"Another incident which I vividly remember at the time of the sinking was about a bloke called Rip Kirby. Now Rip was another torpedo man, and I hardly ever remember him without a tickler in his mouth. He always had a fag dangling from his lips. I knew he was a non-swimmer. However, when I made it to *Impulsive*, I was hauled up the scrambling net and spread out on the upper deck, like a stranded codfish, more dead than alive. After a while, I began to get myself together. The coxswain of *Impulsive* was running around with a jar of rum. He shoved a cup in my hand and filled it up with neat rum. Great, I thought. I must have swallowed a hell of a lot of oil fuel. I took a swig from the cup and thought I was going to be sick. I put my hand over the top of the cup, so that I wouldn't spill any, and spewed over the side. When I'd got rid of some of the oil fuel, I drank the rest of my rum. I then poked my head inside the mess deck and saw Rip Kirby. I couldn't believe my eyes, but there he was with the eternal tickler hanging out of his mouth, and a tot of rum in his hand. 'How the hell did you get over here?' I asked him. 'Well,' he said, 'when I got well up the flight deck, I thought, no good jumping off, you can't swim, and you'll drown. So I sat down and rolled a tickler and thought, right, wait here until the last minute, because it is no good trying to do anything about it.' Well, the ship went down, and down went Kirby with it. Apparently a great bubble of air gushed out of the hangar and Kirby came up inside it. As he shot to the surface spluttering and waving his arms about, there was a lump of wood next to him which he grabbed with both hands. But how the hell a non-swimmer hanging on to a piece of wood could propel himself half a mile through an Atlantic swell and arrive before a strong swimmer, or arrive at all, beats me. I remember washing my hair in a bucket of paraffin to get the oil out of it.

"*Impulsive*'s men were marvellous and did everything they could for us as we were fished out of the water. Some blokes were in a bad way. They gave me a hammock to tie around myself, because all I had on was a very wet undershirt, and the money belt had tightened in the water, and my five quid was as dry as anything. I reckon I was the only survivor of *Courageous* who arrived with five dry quid notes.

"One of the most awful things I remember being told was that the stokers of the last dogwatch were trapped in a lift when the electrics went when the torpedoes exploded. Nobody could help them and they went with the ship. I remember thinking then, what an awful way to go, like rats in a trap.

"I lost many old shipmates and friends, and to this day can't help thinking how unnecessary it all was. Even if the ship had to go, surely in time of war there should have been an issue of life jackets, and more attention given to seeing that life-saving equipment is not only available, but able to be used and freed from its housing. I was myself in the water one and a half hours and only just made it. Without a life jacket non-swimmers and older men had no chance at all."

Petty Officer E G Ballard was an AB on HMS *Inglefield*, the leader of the destroyer escort of *Courageous*. He writes, "We came from the Mediterranean at the outbreak of war and were patrolling the western approaches. Devonport was our base when she was ordered to head the escort group for *Courageous*. As we left harbour we passed *Argus*, an old A/C Carrier fondly known as the old 'floating ditty box', on her way in. We waited outside for *Courageous*, and after the usual exchange of signals took our position ahead of *Courageous*, which we maintained until we were detached with *Intrepid* by order of Capt. Makeig-Jones together with four Swordfish to investigate a report that the SS *Kafiristan* was being gunned by a U-boat on the surface.

"Away we went at speed, and although the weather was pretty good it was bumpy enough in the Atlantic swell, and being at action stations we were pretty keyed up. I remember the first lieutenant doing routine rounds, and after he had been gone a few minutes he returned to tell us that *Courageous* had been torpedoed. Shortly after, we were told that she had sunk, and that we were going back to help search for survivors.

"I shall never forget the scene. A large American liner [SS *Collingsworth*] was picking up survivors and we ourselves had perhaps a hundred or more put aboard us from a small Dutch coaster. A lot of ships had appeared by this time and were doing their utmost to help the victims of this tragedy.

"We stayed at sea for several days, hunting the U-boat that sank *Courageous*, but without success, and by the time we arrived back at 'Guzz' we had little more than iron rations left."

Lt.-Cdr. Ted Collins remembers well that evening fifty years ago, when as a young leading telegraphist he survived the greatest trauma of his young life. He was picked up by *Impulsive* and was in her wireless office when she sent the signal "I am returning with survivors of *Courageous*, in position 040 VDVS.8." which was of course a coded position for 50° 16' N.Lat 14° 5' W, which is 350 miles SW of Ireland, confirmed by the fact that *Impulsive* steamed at almost thirty knots for fifteen hours, to arrive at Plymouth breakwater at 12.30 p.m. on Monday 18th September.

A few years later, he experienced an amazing coincidence when, having been taken prisoner in Crete in 1941, he was in a camp in Austria in 1942. While acting as an interpreter for his fellow prisoners he met a guard who had been invalided out of U-boats; the man turned out to have been a member of the U29 which sank *Courageous*. He told Ted that he didn't know very much about the incident as they got the hell out of it. But he waxed eloquent about their welcome home, when everyone received an Iron Cross.

W G 'Brigham' Young of Birmingham joined the Navy in 1934 and started his service at HMS *St Vincent* and left the RN in '49 as an AB. He joined *Courageous* at Spithead from the Royal Naval Air Station at Eastleigh, HMS *Raven*.

"At the time of the ship being hit we were in the NCOs' Mess below the flight deck, so to get to the upper deck we had to go down the ladder. I remember the incident as if it happened yesterday. We got to the sea boats on the starboard side, and climbed into a motorboat, when all of a sudden somebody yelled, "There's no bloody power on!" I climbed down on the blister and waited until the panic of people throwing planks of wood overboard from the flight deck died down, and then pushed off away from the ship. I was eventually picked up by a tramp steamer.

"I can recall helping a rating up the rope ladder; one of his feet was hanging off. Once on the mess deck someone took the hanging piece right off. God knows what had happened to the poor devil.

"At midnight we were transferred to *Inglefield*, which had come alongside and then steamed into Devonport."

Francis Rogers, a leading cook, joined *Courageous* from HMS *Raven* in August 1939 and had just come off duty when the torpedoes struck and was talking to a young LAC who had just transferred to the FAA. "He was the son of a parson from Devon," he recalls. "He said that they had just come back from bombing submarines and had just landed. No sooner had he said this, there was a terrific bang, and I said to him, 'That must be one of the bombs you left on the plane.' We realised that we had just been torpedoed and both ran up the steps to the catwalk. We could immediately see that the ship was beginning to list nose down on the port side. As the ship started to list more heavily, others of the crew started coming up on deck.

"We were eventually told to abandon ship. I slid down the deck towards the port side, and when the deck was about ten feet from the water I jumped, hoping to grab one of the planks which were floating around. When I surfaced they had disappeared. While I held on to the ship, I saw some men in a motorised boat, still on its davits. They had to wait until the ship pressed the boat into the water so that they could free her from rope falls. Eventually they managed it, and got the boat away and managed to pick up some survivors.

"By this time, I had managed to swim away from the ship and got hold of a plank, and then a jollyboat laden with air tanks, and all its sails intact. I was not alone, there were quite a number of ratings holding on to the side. The sea was getting a little more choppy and as we sat on the edge of the boat it would turn over and we would all be in the water until we righted the boat once more. This happened a number of times, until I put my plank on the windward side and sat on the plank in the water, which kept the boat stable.

"This went on for quite a while until eventually at about 11 p.m. a boat manned by sailors came by and we were picked up and taken aboard a merchant ship which had been making its way home up the western approaches. At about 1 a.m. I was transferred to *Impulsive*.

"Next morning we met up with HMS *Kelly*, Captain, later the Earl, Mountbatten's boat. He wanted to know where we were going. When we told him we were the escort to *Courageous* with survivors going to Devonport, we were told to follow him and do some sub hunting.

"It was 4 p.m. on the Tuesday when we got back to Devonport."

Tom Wright of Cawsand in Cornwall was a member of the RNVR. He was called back into the service in the autumn of 1939, and was sent for two months' training to HMS *Flying Fox* at Bristol.

On completion of his training he was sent to HMS *Drake*, and then to *Courageous*. The ship's company consisted of RNR, RNVR and RFR men, most of whom were well into middle age; a story repeated many times by survivors. "We were going in and out of Plymouth Sound so regularly, at the same time and days each week, that the people of Cawsand were concerned."

These patrols settled more or less into a set pattern once war was declared, and a soldier in the local Ack-Ack garrison was heard to say "Blimey, there she goes again, same time. Why don't they send Adolf a timetable?"

Tom also remembers the yeoman of signals himself making a perforated bag of sail cloth, with brass eyelets, to ensure that it would easily sink. "This was to contain the confidential books." He explained, "I was entrusted with finding a safe place to keep it in case it was needed, so I tied it to the compass binnacle. Little did I think we would need it so soon.

"The order had been given to abandon ship, and I saw Mr Beech the chief yeoman standing on the bridge, looking quite concerned. I asked him what he was going to do, and he told me that he couldn't swim. I learned then that a large number of ratings hadn't been issued with life jackets. I gave him mine as I was a strong swimmer. We helped him over the starboard side, and he was later picked up. By this time the ship had gone down quite a way, bows first, and with a heavy list to port, and it was dangerous to attempt going over the starboard side, so I found a rolled-up length of hose, screwed it to a fire hydrant and rolled it over the flight deck to the water's edge on the port side. On that side, to my dismay there was a lot of oil fuel, and worse still there was a lot of jelly fish; I was stung quite a number of times. I swam away as fast as I could and was picked up by a cargo ship called *Dido* after swimming about for nearly two and a half hours. The *Dido* picked up quite a lot of ratings and two officers, one of them the ship's commander. The destroyer *Kelly* was close by, and sent a signal to the commander, 'I have got a pair of trousers that would fit you.' The captain of *Kelly* was Lord Mountbatten.

"The captain of *Courageous* was last seen helping some ratings over the starboard side. I finally ended up in the RN Barracks and was sent on a month's leave and was afterwards stationed at Rame Head, where I met my wife, who came from nearby Cawsand, and settled there."

Not all that many of the older reservists were as fortunate; many died who should never have been at sea – they should have been ashore with their families.

It is difficult to grasp what would be going through the mind of any individual suddenly faced with such a life-threatening situation as the sinking of a ship. One moment to be safe, in a huge vessel functioning in an everyday routine, doing a job, and then to be in one of the most appalling situations that can be imagined, all within the space of a few seconds. This accounts for some of the apparently conflicting accounts given by survivors.

It is different to just being in action, where you are functioning as a team and have a specific task to carry out; no apparent immediate urgency beyond functioning in the normally accepted way. But from the moment that it becomes apparent that the ship will not survive the damage she has received, then the instinct of self-preservation takes over; every man is basically on his own, with his fears. His world at that moment is encompassed by what he can feel, see and hear. His mind switches over from normal function to the overdrive produced by adrenaline, and the effects of this varies in different people. In some, fear and blind panic, in others apprehension, and in some fatalism, or acceptance of what seems to be the inevitable.

Here we see some of the myriad ways that men were affected and how they coped. In some cases, reason soon took over and the mind came under the control of the will; in some, pure self-preservation, and who can blame them for that? Many prayed and helped themselves; others just prayed. But one thing is certain in the situation that the men of *Courageous* found themselves in: all these emotions must have been there, as they always are in all similar situations, the only slight difference being that this was the Royal Navy's first loss in action for over twenty years. Another very important factor was that the majority of the ship's company had only recently been recalled to the colours, straight from a settled civilian life where there had been no threat to life by war.

All reports indicated that there was no panic, and that the behaviour of the whole ship's company was good, which says a lot for a ship's company who didn't know each other well and had not had time to shake down. But then again, where British people are concerned, self-discipline and stoicism are the rule rather than the exception, and that is a matter of historic fact.

Another crew member vividly remembers that fateful day. He remembers the last patrol, when the ship left Plymouth early in the morning on 16th September. "The captain spoke to the ship's company over the tannoy saying that we would be hunting enemy submarines known to be operating in the area, and that 'everyone must be on their toes or the hunter would become the hunted'. How prophetic those words were to be." He remembers the beautiful September day and that he had been assisting in the flying off and landing of the aircraft which had been patrolling. "From 6-8 p.m., the last dogwatch, I had been off duty; we had had our evening meal, and I was due on watch at 2000 hours as one of the crew of the gun on the fo'c'sle. Two of us went to the fo'c'sle early to enjoy a smoke while it was still daylight, and were in time to see the last of our aircraft land, and the ship, which had turned into the wind for the landing, altered course to proceed on the normal patrol course. No sooner had she finished turning, the torpedoes struck just forward of amidships. Immediately the ship took on a very heavy list to port, and we learned that all lights in the ship went out. There was no doubt that this added to the very heavy loss of life.

"Several of us attempted to release a raft – I do not think it was a Carley float – but this had been well secured for years, and periodically painted. We found this not possible without tools. We then realised that the port side was almost under water. We took off our shoes and most of our clothing and walked into the water. The only boat that I saw get away was a motorboat and that was quite crowded. I obtained a piece of wood, which probably saved my life.

"*Courageous* went down bows first, and the last I saw of her was the four great screws still turning as the stern came out of the water. I was picked up by a merchant ship bound for Liverpool, whose crew supplied us with clothing and warm food. Early next morning *Intrepid* came alongside and embarked us, and we returned to the RN Barracks at Devonport.

"At that time I was thirty-six years of age, an able seaman. Many of the ship's company were pensioners, who ought not to have been at sea. The ship was seaworthy, but the life-saving equipment was nil. In peacetime it is what a ship looks like that matters, and it is easy to practise abandon ship when it is on even keel, but not so easy when there is a heavy list. We were not then the Royal Navy at war. History repeated itself and we went into the war as if it were a game."

An awesome price was paid by the men of our services for the stupidity and ineptitude of those in high places between the world wars. The price was paid in blood, grief, and the misery of those who in the main had nothing to do with the planning and strategy of our armed services. In all too many cases the real culprits emerged from the conflict scot-free and smelling of roses. And in many cases with very much enhanced incomes and often undeserved status.

Ronald Bell was a young signalman at the time of the sinking of *Courageous*, and takes up the story. "It is a long time ago now, and we had only been commissioned a few weeks. I can only remember the name of my leading signalman, a man from Liverpool recalled from the reserve, named Green. He had, I remember, two daughters of whom he spoke often.

"Although I was part of the original ship's company to commission *Courageous* in Devonport, I am only a technical survivor for, together with another signalman, I was recalled to HMS *Drake*, and we both left the ship with our kitbags and hammocks on the very last time that she was in harbour in Portland where she embarked aircraft.

"Something like a third of the ship's company were RNVR, young lads from London offices, farm boys, young men from the major cities, mining lads from Scotland and Yorkshire; a mixed bag of nice ordinary young men, little aware that soon their lives would be forfeit, and many non-swimmers among them.

"I agree with the survivor who spoke of the 'terrible waste!' But let us honour those good men who died by recognising that Britain did not seek their death through war. As the Munich agreement and betrayal of the Czechs demonstrated, Britain feared and tried to avoid war. It takes two to make peace, and surely our shipmates did not die for nothing.

"It is sad, and a little uncanny, to stand on the Hoe in Plymouth by the Naval war memorial, and see the place where your own name was so nearly embossed. My eye falls down the long list, and suddenly, a name becomes a face, and I see a man as I knew him. Strange it is that so many years make us forget names, but not faces. No, I do not think that *Courageous* was ill-prepared. Bearing in mind the oh-so-short time she had to gird her loins for battle she was as well prepared as was possible, given the time she had for training and exercises at sea. She was unfortunate to be, so early in the war, the victim of a brilliant and determined attack. I know that, but for the fortunes of war, she would have been a happy ship, and would have given a good account of herself."

Tansey Lee, a leading telegraphist in *Ivanhoe*, one of the two destroyer escorts left with *Courageous* at the time of the sinking, remembers, "We did not pick up any survivors, as we were busy chasing Asdic contacts with the submarine. I remember that just after *Courageous* was hit we took evasive action as two torpedoes headed in our direction. I was on the signal deck and saw those fish quite distinctly and remember vividly getting a grip on the rails, and saying to myself, 'If the ship goes up, I'm not going with her.' I have always had the idea that we were more lucky than we appeared to be at the time, and that they shot off on another tack which saved us more than our hard over wheel."

In fact, it is more likely that Tansy Lee saw two of the three torpedoes that Schuhart fired and remembered that two of the three hit *Courageous*. Nobody was aware of U29's presence until the torpedoes actually struck, and at that moment *Courageous* was on the turn, having just landed aircraft. Also *Ivanhoe* and *Impulsive* were a thousand yards on either bow. So the torpedoes would have passed very close to *Ivanhoe*.

Jack (Nutty) Rowntree, an RAF corporal fitter, one of the many RAF men aboard *Courageous* tells his story.

"I joined the RAF in March 1937 and along with a pal of mine, 'Nobby' Clarke, was posted to Donibristle, a Fleet Air Arm shore base on the Firth of Forth. From there we used to practise deck landings on the carrier *Furious* and it was quite a novelty after the runways in the RAF, but the novelty was soon to disappear with my next drafting. I think it was Sunday, 2nd September, my mate and I were in the Mess Hall having our tea when in came a PO and started reeling off names, about a hundred or more, and telling us to get our kits packed and be ready to catch the train, which was about 20.00 hours from Inverkeithing. My mate was not on the list.

"We eventually got down to Lee-on-Solent hours late, only to find that the carrier *Courageous* had left and gone down to Portland with the draft meant for the *Albatross*, so most of our blokes went to the *Albatross* and the rest, about twenty-seven of us, including me, started chasing between Portland and Plymouth, eventually catching and boarding the *Courageous* at Plymouth. They didn't hang around very long, for we no sooner got settled in when we were ordered out and did a week's patrol, then back to Plymouth again for the weekend.

"I went to the cinema on the Friday evening and halfway through the show it was flashed up on the screen for all personnel of *Courageous* to report back immediately, and we set sail that evening. It was on the following evening, Sunday 17th September, that we were 'tin-fished'.

"It was supper time and I was cook-o-the-mess with another bloke, meaning that it was our turn to dish up the grub and wash up the dishes afterwards. He had finished his meal and was down on the gun deck having a smoke when I went down after collecting the dishes together and, passing him on the way up again, said I would be up in a tick to give him a hand. There were quite a few of us there, FAA ratings, and I was sitting on one of the piano stools on the gun platform and we were commenting on a small coaster off the starboard side. The ship had just swung into wind and was handing on 'Kites' after patrol.

"All of a sudden there was one almighty explosion followed almost immediately by a second and a similar third one. Someone suggested it might be the water condensers or the boiler had blown but when the ship started to keel over and one or two blokes came through from the fo'c'sle covered in oil, etc., and their gear almost torn from their backs, it was time for second thoughts. Then a rating came along the deck from aft, telling us not to hang around as we had been torpedoed. That was it, everybody panicked, including me, and up the hatch I went, hoping to get on to the flight deck. The landing was packed with ratings from the mess deck and in the middle was a chief baker who had a torch, as all the electrics had gone. He was trying to get some sort of order but he was wasting his time. I didn't hang about, back down the hatchway I went and along the deck then up an outer hatchway to the top deck only to find my way barred by a 'Tubby Man' sick berth attendant. He wouldn't let me through so down I came again following a PO or chief cook. On reaching the gun deck two blokes shouted for me to come along there as they had a rope over the side, but the rope wasn't needed as the ship was so far over by then it was just a case of sliding down on my backside.

"By the way, all this happened in just a few minutes, such was the panic, and although we knew war had been declared, I don't think we realised just how quick it was going to catch us up. I for one didn't.

"Just below the waterline on the ship was what I think is called a bilge keel, then almost on the bottom itself is another, about 6-8" square section, and it was on this lower one that I was standing with the water lapping my feet when another RAF bloke joined me. We exchanged a few comments then he asked, 'What happens when you can't swim?' to which I replied, 'Don't ask me, mate! It takes all my time to swim a width of the baths at home and it is a bloody long way to that destroyer over there.' With that, we stripped, me to my underwear and socks, and in he went first, and as I watched he grabbed a red wooden chock used on aircraft wheels and seemed to be OK, then it was my turn and in I went.

"As my hand came out of the water it touched something which I grabbed, it was a piece of wood like you would get in a bundle of chopsticks for the fire. Then it dawned on me that my feet wouldn't stay up, they were too heavy with the thick woolly socks full of water, so I had to struggle to get rid of them. Turning on my back after that to see what was going on, I saw the red chock but no one on it, so whether it was the same one or not and he had gone under, it is hard to say, but I never saw him any more. Then it was off for me, still hanging on to my piece of wood like grim death. On the way across I had to keep turning on my back to rest and with the huge swell that was running I could see all around me one minute and there seemed to be lots of bodies floating bottoms up and quite a few swimming as well. Then I was down in the dip and couldn't see anything. On one occasion when on my back the carrier seemed to be further over than ever, then all of a sudden it righted itself and started to slowly dive into the depths, bow first. It was then I noticed all the blokes scrambling up towards the stern trying to get away from the water, some of them were jumping or being pushed over the stern, I don't know, but the ship slowly disappeared beneath the swell. After a few moments, out of the water shot one of the ship's booms, like an arrow, they used to be slung from the hangar deckhead for storage. I remember thinking, God help anybody underneath when it comes down.

"Away again, and as we got nearer the destroyer HMS *Impulsive*, she lowered the boats and began picking us up and, funnily enough, one of the blokes who was being hauled in the cutter with me was a marine by the name of Kit Taylor who came from my home of Ashington, and I almost married his cousin Peggy Taylor, but that is something else.

"When we got alongside the destroyer, the swell made it so that I was looking up on her deck one moment, then way down below the next so I decided to grab the rail next time up and haul myself on board, but didn't have the strength. Two pairs of welcome hands came over and grabbed my wrists and lifted me right over onto the deck where I was told to get below and get some dry clothing and something hot to drink.

"Before I go any further, I've got to say this about the crew aboard the *Impulsive*. They were great, throwing open their kitbags, lockers and hammocks and distributing their gear right, left and centre, so that everyone had something to put on even if it was only a towel to wrap around. This was comradeship in the navy in those days. There were one or two dead bodies lying in one of the messes on tables but whether they died on the way across or after they got on board, I don't know but I do know there was lots of oil on the water as was apparent the moment I looked in the mirror, but the blokes who came in after me were a lot worse, so these bodies could have been suffocated, who knows, I don't.

"As the time went on there was a tannoy message to say that they were going to search for another half an hour then off home to Plymouth. It was almost midnight.

"We arrived in Plymouth early the following morning and a more bedraggled lot you never saw. It was wet and cold and we were lined up on the road garbed in anything we had managed to get. The most embarrassing thing was the civilian staff coming in to work, they just stood there goggling as if we were German prisoners or something. Eventually we were allowed home on survivors' leave and I got home to find that the news of the sinking had not only shook my family to their roots but had almost killed my mother, 'cos out of four brothers, two were too young and the eldest was down the mine like my dad, meaning I was the only one away.

"After returning from leave I was drafted to HMS *Hermes*, another carrier, but that's another story.

"By the way, if you are wondering if there were any life jackets, at least I never saw any except on Kit Taylor, the marine previously mentioned, and I think that is why later all ships crew were issued with their own inflatables to carry around.

"It's all something to remember, I suppose."

Commander (Air) Dan Baker was the senior observer in *Courageous* at the time of the sinking. He was the most senior surviving officer that I have been able to contact.

I was surprised to learn that Commander Baker had not been called to give evidence at the Board of Inquiry, and indeed never knew when it had taken place. This seems all the more strange in view of the fact that it was his job to advise the captain on all matters to do with flying and the air situation at any time. In view of the fact that *Courageous* was hit following a series of movements and speed changes involved in landing on aircraft, and it was considered that this was one of the factors contributing to the sinking, I find this most strange.

Commander Baker described Captain Makeig-Jones as "a lovely man", and had served with him previously in another carrier HMS *Furious*, when he was executive officer, and Commander Baker commanded a wing. Both were keen boxers – Makeig-Jones had been three times a Royal Navy heavyweight champion. He remembered the moment that the torpedoes struck, just as *Courageous* came out of the turn. The ship had still been turning as the last aircraft landed. The timing could not have been worse – just on the change of watch, and as the ship's movements had been dictated by the landing on of aircraft rather than by the necessity of her own security. Captain Makeig-Jones was remembered to have remarked immediately, "That was a damned fine shot." It was typical of this fine man that in such a situation he could pay tribute to another professional.

Because of the noise of the siren, shouted orders were almost impossible to hear from a distance of more than a few feet. On the bridge it was obvious that there was little that could be done to save the ship; she was doomed from the moment of impact. Commander Abel-Smith, the executive officer, (Commander Baker knew him well) went on to command the Royal Yacht. He was told by the captain to pass the order to abandon ship.

Commander Baker remembers stripping down to his underpants and leaving the ship from the starboard quarter. He swam to a Carley float, one of the few that could be launched. It was so loaded that men were standing on it and their heads were only just above the water. He ordered swimmers off in order to let non-swimmers on, and got blank stares. He remarked many years after, "In a situation like that you can't expect a man to obey such an order when he thinks he may die if he does what you tell him."

He was eventually picked up, and next morning, aboard *Inglefield*, steaming around looking for any possible survivors, he remembers seeing many men, with life jackets, their heads above water, dead. He couldn't understand why at the time, but it was generally accepted that the tremendous repercussion of the depth charges dropped by *Ivanhoe* had resulted in the death of so many. As one survivor said, "How ironic to escape from a sinking ship to be killed in the water like that." He paused and then said, "But I think I'd rather go that way than to be trapped inside her."

Commander Baker went on, "The ship was in no way worked up. We had only been commissioned two months and the ship's company had hardly had time to get to know each other." This statement was something which was to be repeated many times in accounts given by survivors. He continued, "There was some timber floating in the water, but there was almost a total absence of life-saving equipment." It is certain that, although some men had them, there had been no general issue of life jackets.

This in itself must have resulted in many deaths among non-swimmers, and it is difficult to understand why this obvious lack of thought for the safety of men in such situations was not remedied. There must surely have been somebody responsible for assessing and checking safety factors as elementary as these. One wonders whether aircrew members all had parachutes at this stage of the war. There could surely be no difference. One has to ask, how contemptuous was the Admiralty for human life.

There were many men in the service in those times from Southern Ireland, many of whom had served in the First World War in *Courageous*. A number of them were drinking in the Free State, a public house in Devonport, on the last evening before she sailed on that last fateful voyage. The conversation began to flag and a feeling of terrible foreboding came over the group, a feeling which could not but have been felt by them all and brought an end to the previous banter.

This was not the only incidence of dreadful foreboding associated with the *Courageous* sinking. It is strange that in so many instances of danger and disaster, many people have these inexplicable feelings of impending tragedy and misfortune, particularly in connection with such situations at sea.

My mother was one of those who shared this feeling of imminent calamity; the only difference being that it was almost at the moment that the *Courageous* was struck. The evening was one of exceptional beauty - warm, bright and balmy. My brother and I were with her, enjoying the lovely walk along Vicarage Road, St Budeaux, which at its end looked over the Tamar towards Saltash and Cornwall. The sun was low over the west and the evening sky was orange red. The same sky and same colours that formed the backdrop at the scene of the sinking, and through Schuhart's periscope. We were all enjoying this beautiful autumn evening, the hedgerows and view over the fields and the river. I can see my mother now, in her navy blue summer frock and broad-brimmed hat. She suddenly stopped and shuddered, her expression one of shock, and her face like chalk. She remained still for some seconds, and quietly, almost in a whisper said "Oh my God, something awful has happened." I can only remember that we walked home in silence. I can remember the incident distinctly, and in some childish way the feeling it imparted to me. A few minutes later, the clock at the naval barracks struck eight. My parents were very close and shared everything, and I am sure that she knew at that moment that what had happened had involved my father.

The sinking was well publicised in Eire and considerable coverage was given by the *Cork Examiner*, which ran many stories from survivors, and indeed seemed to have carried the story with a more human presentation than did the English newspapers. The English papers printed bold headlines, and cold facts, which, it could be argued, is the purpose of a newspaper, but the effect is often painful, and sadly lacking in human sensitivity to the point of being cruel to those who are already in a state of grief-induced shock.

Perhaps Eire, being a smaller country with a vastly smaller population, mainly in smaller communities, which are close-knit by family ties, had a more sympathetic approach and human understanding than our press, even in those days.

A long list of men who at the time were presumed missing, or were reported dead, appeared in the *Examiner*: a man from Whitegate – no news at present. Another from Middleton safe. Yet another from Skibbereen – officially stated to be dead. The list grows of men from Waterford, Macroom, Dungarvan, Cork, Rosscarbery and

Ballycotton. A retired petty officer who had served in the First World War was notified of the death of his son, who had served seven years and had been on leave only a week before the outbreak of war, three weeks before the sinking. A local newsagent whose son was reported dead – the boy was twenty-one. A man who was torpedoed three times in the First World War bore a charmed life – he survived yet again.

A chief petty officer from Middleton told the story of his own escape from the doomed ship. "I was sitting on the deck enjoying a cigarette on this lovely sunny evening when, with another chief, we heard the explosions. He said, 'By God, that's us.' We went to the hangar in inky darkness, and unfortunately I got caught in the hangar door. It was no easy job to extricate myself because the ship had a heavy list to port. Following some upheaval, I was thrown on to the upper hangar, and collided with the tail end of a torpedo. I eventually succeeded in getting through to the starboard side and then to the flight deck. The next thing I heard was the order to abandon ship, and getting rid of everything I had on, I dived some 80-90ft into blackness, luckily escaping the ship's bulges, the cause I believe of so many lives being lost. I was two hours and twenty-seven minutes in the water, swimming as best I could, and catching hold of any wreckage afloat at the time. I eventually became unconscious, and remembered nothing until I was picked up by the *Impulsive*, to the members of which crew I owe a deep debt of gratitude.

"I remember hearing some of the men singing, 'Where the Blarney roses grow', when I was in the water. To my mind this was a great tonic to men who were fighting for their lives."

It can well be imagined that men would be affected by a song in such extreme conditions, the evocative link with home which can move a man to greater efforts to save himself, even if he is too far spent to survive, at least to depart life hearing voices raised in a song of home.

The spirit of many of these Irishmen could only be described as remarkable, and many instances of courage and endurance were recorded in the *Cork Examiner* as told by survivors. Mr Ronayne, another survivor, had been torpedoed four times: three times in the first war and now *Courageous*. Who can possibly imagine the state of mind of someone finding themselves in such a situation, high up on a towering flight deck of an aircraft-carrier, knowing that you have only a few minutes to get off the ship, a task in itself fraught with peril.

How do you get off? On the port side the list is such that if you jump, you would very possibly have the ship roll on top of you if she took a sudden roll; she took on a 15°–20° list immediately she was hit. Also as the fuel tanks had been ripped open the water was full of oil on that side of the ship, and when you surfaced, you would be covered in the awful goo and probably have your vision impaired. If you got that far, then you had to make your way over to a rescue ship.

If you were on the starboard side, then the list to port was so great that to dive off the upper or lower flight deck would almost certainly have resulted in serious injury, as it did in some cases of men being horribly injured by hitting the bulges; also the list was steadily increasing all the time. To slide down the ship's side was also fraught with serious problems. To slide down facing the ship would mean serious injuries to the face possibly, the stomach and genitals certainly, if a man slipped and gained momentum not being able to control the rate of slide with his hands owing to the slimy underside of the bulges, and the barnacles and marine growth. The best option was with his back to the ship's side and using hands and legs to carefully regulate a slow descent. As one survivor said, "Better a battered and torn bum than lacerated nuptials." And that is only getting as far as the water. Next comes swimming prowess. It is amazing how many sailors cannot swim at all, and many that can are a long way short of Olympic standards. The non-swimmers were not just junior ratings: many were older men, some chiefs and petty officers. Swimming ability was, however, assessed each time you spent a period in the barracks at your port division, Devonport, Portsmouth or Chatham, at the same time as you went through what was known as the "Joining ship routine". Everyone had to have his chitty signed by the medical officer and dental surgeon, get his inoculations up to date, and pay a visit to the gymnasium and swimming bath.

Ed Connally of Ballycotton was a veteran of the First World War, fifty-two years of age, and esteemed by all his friends and acquaintances. He had a wife and an aged mother, whose youngest son was drowned at the beginning of the first war. A remarkable coincidence was that both brothers lost their lives on the same date in September, twenty-five years apart. Edward, always a happy jovial man, was an auxiliary relief to the men on Ballycotton Lighthouse.

From Rosscarbery, Michael McCarthy aged twenty-five, had served in the Navy for seven years as an air mechanic, and had been on leave only three weeks before the sinking, and was like many others, recalled. His father was a retired petty officer.

Joseph Brunt, twenty-one, of Waterford, an engineer, whose mother was a newsagent, lost his life. Patrick Duggan of Cork perished, leaving a young widow. She spent nearly three days of torture after she wired the Admiralty, and received no reply, growing more anxious each day as she watched the list of survivors for his name. But it did not appear. They had lived in Middlesex until the outbreak of war, when she and her daughter went to live in Cork.

Another survivor was forty-five-year-old William Britton of Glasgow, a Stoker with twenty-three years' service in the RN. Back in his home after the ordeal he showed his watch, the hands stopped at six minutes past eight. He told a reporter that it was a cheap watch, but had become his most treasured possession. Six minutes past eight was the time when he had dived into the sea from *Courageous* on that awesome evening, and could well have told the time of his death. With a young seaman from Dunbarton, Andrew Logue, he told of a PO on one of the rescue destroyers who dived many times into the sea to rescue men who were exhausted, and held them until they could be lifted inboard, and a young AB who twice dived in to rescue men who were near the end of their endurance.

Stoker Britton was playing rummy when the torpedoes struck. One of the players had left to go on watch; there were about fifty men on the mess deck at that time, mostly talking or writing letters. Within seconds he was up to his neck in water. They groped about in complete darkness and felt their way to the upper deck. He said that he didn't think that twelve of them got out. He saw a boat full of men and struck out for her, but she foundered before he reached her. He said, "I then saw a destroyer and turned and swam towards her and was picked up. You cannot speak too highly of the fine work done by the rescue boats. I have been tasting oil fuel from the water ever since. We were all sick from the stuff we had swallowed."

Another stoker, although badly burned and covered with oil fuel thought of his comrades, "What are the lads below doing – what about them?" More fortunate was a Dungarvan man, Patrick Curran, whose invalid mother was not aware that her son's ship had been torpedoed, and was only aware of the sinking when she received a letter from her son. He was well, apart from suffering shock.

There were many reports in the Press at that time that the U-boat had been sunk, but there was never any real reason to believe that it had. All these accounts were soon proved wrong when reports that she had returned to Germany in triumph were later proved right.

Leading stoker Michael Fleming of Cork had gone up to the promenade deck for a smoke before doing his rounds. He was nearly deafened and blinded by the explosion and thought at first that it was a depth charge. But when the ship took a huge list to port he realised what had happened as the promenade deck flooded. He swam under water in the direction he hoped was aft. The flight deck on the port side was only a couple of feet above water and people on the flight deck were lowering chains so that men below could climb up. Hoping that he would be able to get over to the starboard side and perhaps help in lowering boats he climbed up, but found that none of the boats could be lowered because of the loss of power and the angle of list being so great as to make it impossible to lower a boat without it hitting the side and capsizing. He managed to get into the water and grab an oar, but a seaman near him pleaded, "Give me a hand, I'm beat"; being able to swim he gave him the oar, but feared he was drowned because he didn't see him afterwards. He was two-and-a-half hours swimming before he was picked up by the destroyer. Another Cork man that he knew was on watch at the time of the hit, but he was sure that he didn't get out because many of the ladders from compartments were dislodged by the vibration of the explosion or by being dislodged when the ship listed so heavily.

George Roseveare was a young Royal Marine and commander's runner at the time when the torpedoes struck, and remarked that it could not have been at a worse time: the changing of the watch. He recalls, "I was standing next to surgeon Commander Brown at that moment, and wondered what the devil had happened. *Ivanhoe*, on our port side immediately shot off and started depth charging around the area where it was thought the U-boat was. By this time, quite a few men were in the water, and you can imagine the effect this had on those left on board. The depth charging went on for some time; thankfully it gradually decreased near to the ship, but many were killed by the shock pressure." George also attested to the lack of life-saving equipment, and the fact that only one or two boats could be launched and Carley floats couldn't be dislodged from the mountings.

When he got into the water, his eyes were badly affected by oil fuel. He swam away from the side of the ship, coming near to a chief and several men hanging on to a plank; he went on, "I could see that it couldn't support all of them so I kept away. My eyes were gummed up with oil, and I literally had to prise them open to see where I was, and take a look around. Some time later a boat came near, and I saw a man standing in it, a Sergeant Williams. He told me that I couldn't come aboard as it was already overcrowded, but told me to hang on to the side. I did, and they took me over to *Intrepid*, which had nets over the side. I had hurt my ribs and side, and had lost the top of one of my fingers. I don't know how.

"I was helped up the scrambling net, and joined the other poor devils who were retching up oil fuel. They shoved a tube down your throat and pumped some of the fuel oil out and tried to make you sick. I had arrived on board without a stitch on, and someone gave me a pair of pyjamas and a pair of dungarees, and three of us were sent down to the engine room platform for warmth. I was told that a warning was sent out that no other ships were to enter the zone. We left at midnight or thereabouts. If I remember rightly we went like the clappers of hell, and got into Plymouth early Monday afternoon. The men aboard *Impulsive* were fantastic, and did everything they could to help us."

Strangely enough, George later went on to become a pilot. It appears that at that time anyone who had the desire and aptitude to fly could volunteer. He said that he felt sure that this was because it was so risky at that time that only a fool would volunteer.

There are times when comedy enters on the scene and almost makes a farce of tragedy. Such a time occurred aboard *Impulsive* when the survivors were hauled up from the sea by willing hands, many after their half-mile swim, shocked and near exhaustion; some left on the deck to recover a little while rescuers fought to bring others aboard. After coughing up some of the oil fuel, and beginning to move around, they were moved into the various mess decks, whenever there was room. Once there they were given tea and rum, which often encouraged vomiting, which cleared some of the oil fuel from their stomachs. One of *Impulsive*'s crew members related the story of one of the survivors who had all but given up, and found himself drifting off into a sleep. He said, "I don't know why, but I caught myself dozing off, and I jerked awake choking with seawater. I suddenly remembered being told that in those situations you must guard against sleep. After a while it happened again, and this time it really scared me, and God knows why I should have thought such a thing, but the thought suddenly entered my head, if you drop off you'll drown and Nellie will never have another new hat!" It appears that his wife Nellie had an awful habit of buying new hats every week or two, and it was a sort of compulsion. It is perhaps the first time a man was saved from drowning by his wife's compulsive millinery fetish.

From the moment that the torpedoes struck, all was activity. First there were frantic efforts to save the ship, because all sailors know that she is the safest lifebelt, their best chance, and every effort is made to save her. Everyone acts as a team where possible. But when it is no longer possible to keep the ship afloat, the primary objective is to save oneself, and every effort is directed towards that one aim. This is not to say that the order of the day is selfishness, because nothing could be further from the truth, and there are far too many acts of heroism for there to be any doubt to the contrary. But once the ship has gone there is a complete change of feeling. There is no longer a common focal point.

To begin with, there is a strange silence. While a ship is afloat there is a sort of heartbeat; a throbbing, as if from a beating heart. It is real. Even though she may be mortally wounded, one can still hear sounds within her body; her boilers may still be working even though losing pressure; things may be moving around inside her, perhaps caused by the list or motion of the sea or gear breaking adrift. In the case of *Courageous* her siren bellowed almost as soon as she was hit, and continued until she disappeared. When eventually she disappeared from view, these sounds ceased after a final crescendo caused by her inside almost falling apart, or perhaps a boiler bursting and bulkheads finally giving way. In the case of *Courageous* she was already down by the head and listing over 45° when she began to go under with a slowly increasing speed until, with her screws still turning, she disappeared in a mass of foam and uprush of air and buoyant gear detaching itself and shooting to the surface. At that moment there is a strange silence which is almost eerie, and can only be likened to the last moments of a dying human.

A marshalling of strength, a quickening of breathing, a final deep sigh, and then... peace.

It is then that there is a pause, and eyes seem to be glued to the place where she was, and there is a feeling of utter disbelief, and then a sense of loss approaching grief, because sailors do grieve for their ships, and never forget them. It is then that another emotion takes over - vulnerability. Men are in the water, more often than not naked, and the vastness of the sea invades their consciousness to an extent that it takes all their inner strength to stave off panic.

At the moment of the torpedo strike the only ships near were *Ivanhoe* and *Impulsive*. *Ivanhoe* immediately ordered *Impulsive* to stand by *Courageous*, and herself raced around attempting to make contact with the U-boat. The first patterns of depth charges were fairly wide of the mark, and it was fairly certain that many men in the water suffered very severely from the shock; many men saying that there were bodies floating face down in the water. Worse still, a few who did have life jackets were floating in an upright position, but with their faces in the water.

There had been no general issue of life jackets, so it was all the more 'ironic' that men who would almost certainly have survived should have been killed by depth charging.

It was not long before there were some other ships on the scene. The first was the SS *Collingsworth*, an American steamer, very possibly the one that Schuhart saw through his periscope at 1617 hours, but we cannot be sure. She rendered valuable assistance in picking up four officers and thirty-four men. Also, the SS *Van Deem*, a Dutch vessel, took some survivors aboard, one of whom died afterwards. The others were taken off later when HMS *Kelly* came on the scene. Her captain was Lord Louis Mountbatten.

The Board of Inquiry made particular mention of the master, officers and men of the SS *Dido* which stopped en route from Alexandria to Liverpool to assist, for their prompt action and disregard for their own safety. They saved many lives. The master put his ship at the disposal of the survivors, which involved very considerable private expense in parting with clothing etc. It is believed that she took on nearly three hundred survivors.

The risk taken by all the ships who rendered aid was very considerable when it was known that there was a U-boat still in the vicinity, but such is the comradeship of the sea, and such conduct, thank God, is the rule rather than the exception; indeed there are even numerous instances of enemies stopping to aid survivors in circumstances which have laid them open to great danger.

Chapter Eleven

If

One of the smallest words in our language, yet the one word which leads the mind on to its greatest journeys.

The *Courageous* tragedy is so charged with ifs that any one of them could result in a very different story with a very different ending. It would be impossible to deal with all the ifs in any sort of sequence because few people would agree as to the right sequence. So I will try and deal with them in the order in which they occur to me.

The first is that, although *Courageous* was basically very seaworthy, she was by wartime standards very old, over twenty years old, and was never designed originally to do the job that she did so well for most of her service life. The one thing that she and her sisters shared was a tremendously high turn of speed – always an advantage in a carrier. But she did have one big fault, one which perhaps more than any other single factor contributed more to her rapid sinking and heavy loss of life once the torpedoes struck, and that was that her ring main (electrical circuit) was not split, and once severed, there was no electrical power throughout this massive ship. This resulted in complete darkness below, and complete loss of all communications, so that no orders could be given apart from very limited verbal commands and instructions. The other result was that apart from one seaboat, lowered by rope falls, none of the other boats could be lowered because they were operated by electrical current. Much time was spent and energy wasted in trying to release boats.

Probably the next most costly factor in terms of loss of life was that there was no general issue of life jackets to the ship's company. It is true that some men did have jackets, but as far as can be ascertained they were their own property, and not naval issue. Not much was made of this at the time, but it would be difficult to imagine the MOD getting away with that today. So, if there had been electrical current, there would have been some sort of secondary lighting and men would have had a far better chance of getting out from below and off the ship. The group of stokers trapped in a lift would have survived, and orders could have been transmitted which would have almost certainly helped with damage control and perhaps resulted in the ship staying afloat long enough to have saved more lives, even if the ship could not have been ultimately saved. Remember, she sank nineteen minutes after the torpedoes struck.

Another factor which contributed to the heavy loss of life was that steel ladders in compartments were not properly secured and swung upwards when the ship heeled over, thereby trapping men. It was recommended by the Board of Inquiry that they should in future be secured in the down position so that they could not swing up when the ship heels over.

There were repeated instances reported of Carley floats being stuck to their mountings by the accumulation of years of continued painting; this too was mentioned in the Inquiry. "The stowage of Carley floats should be given attention at once, and none which are slung should rest in brackets. They should be slung clear of obstacles with the weight taken by a tackle and bowsed in and secured with a lashing."

I first contacted Kapt. Schuhart in 1982, when I started to research the sinking of *Courageous*, and it was with a little apprehension that I first wrote him asking if he would be prepared to help me in my task. This was the first step on a road which led to us corresponding for eight years, and meeting in 1989, only a few months before his death. He described his early successes: *The Regent Tiger* on 8th June, and on 12th June he stopped the high sea tug *Neptunia*, intending to sink her by torpedo and test the new magnetic ignition-system which was unfamiliar to him. The torpedo detonated before the bow of U29, and the second before the target. He says, "Something must be wrong! I give orders to shift the ignition system, and we used in future the old impact system. In fact, the magnetic system was not enough proved and was faulty, and must be corrected before in 1940 it was safe. It has cost us many successes and one submarine."

What he was referring to was the sinking of the U39 on 14th September, when the *Ark Royal*, with an escort of three destroyers, *Faulknor*, *Foxhound* and *Firedrake*, acting as a screen, was carrying out anti-submarine exercises off the west coast of Scotland. Three other destroyers, *Tartar*, *Bedouin* and *Punjab*, had been detached to go ahead to a position where the SS *Fanad Head* had been attacked by a U-boat about 180 miles to the south westward. At 1432*Ark Royal* turned into the wind to fly off three "Skuas" whilst the destroyers maintained their course and speed. *Ark Royal* turned back after the aircraft had flown off and was about four miles astern of the screen at 1507. When *Ark Royal* was about two miles astern of the screen, U39 fired two torpedoes at her, both of which missed astern and exploded in her wake. The speed of *Ark Royal* had been estimated at twenty-two knots but she was really doing twenty-six. U39 had passed within three thousand yards of the nearest destroyer, and hearing the explosions thought that she had scored a hit. The destroyers turned back, and two thousand yards apart searched to the north-westward of the *Ark Royal*. They soon picked up a contact. *Foxhound* attacked at once and dropped two depth charges.

U39 had dived deep as soon as she saw the destroyers coming it her, and at the time of the first attack was only at about 230 feet. The attack put the lights out and damaged the main battery. The main electric motors were also put out of action by the short circuiting caused by flooding. *Faulknor* followed with another attack, and a full pattern of depth charges was dropped. This caused more leaks in the boat. Firedrake carried out a formal attack with depth charges set to 250–500 feet. This did most damage and water started pouring in. The U-boat was by now quite out of control, and was filling with chlorine. Almost immediately U39 broke surface and all three destroyers opened fire. When it was seen that the crew were abandoning ship fire was checked. All forty-three crew escaped through the conning tower wearing lifebelts, but not before assuring that U39 would sink.

There were several things worth noting at this point, one being that all the U-boat crew wore lifebelts. Why was there no general issue of lifebelts or jackets to the ship's company of *Courageous*? We now come to another *if*. Schuhart, as soon as he experienced the failure of the magnetic torpedoes, warned all the other boats, including U39, and told me that he could never understand why the commander of U39 ignored him, but said that years later he had admitted that he regretted the failure to learn from Schuhart's experience. As a U-boat ace said to a group of newcomers to the U-boat Arm: "There's one thing you can't do in a U-boat. You can't profit from your mistakes.

You don't live long enough." If he had listened, *Ark Royal* would probably have been a victim, and if Schuhart hadn't experienced the failure of magnetic torpedoes with *Neptunia*, he would possibly have used them on *Courageous* and suffered the same fate as U39, and *Courageous* would not have fallen victim.

Most importantly, if the Admiralty had learned from the attack on *Ark Royal* on the 14th, then *Courageous* would not have been lost. *Ark Royal* was at her most vulnerable when she despatched aircraft and half her escort to go to the aid of *Fanad Head* following an SOS, and was manoeuvring to fly off aircraft. To do this, the carrier has to increase speed and cease "zigzagging", presenting a perfect target to a U-boat. Why, when this had already nearly lost *Ark Royal*, did the Admiralty not immediately abandon these so obviously vulnerable anti-submarine hunting groups? Besides, *Courageous* had only four destroyers, and *Ark Royal* had six. It was mentioned in the report of the Board of Inquiry that "at 1630 *Courageous* flew on the three patrolling aircraft (which had been recalled) and at 1645 proceeded at twenty-three knots on course 275° to close towards the reported position of the submarine, and so lessen the return distance of the air striking force. The reason for this was the incomplete state of training of the observers who frequently failed to find the carrier. On this occasion two of the four did become lost and had to be given D/F bearings to be got back. This fact was mentioned in the inquiry, and also by Lt.-Cdr. Lamb who was the pilot of the last Swordfish to land only a minute or so before the torpedoes struck. From this time, no A/S air patrol was maintained, the reason being that because of the incompleteness of training the captain did not wish to have too many aircraft in the air at one time." Nobody could possibly blame Captain Makeig-Jones for this. He had a straight choice: have too many aircraft in the air with observers whose training was incomplete and who frequently got lost, resulting in his having to go and look for them – in itself a dangerous exercise – or just rely on his fairly high speed by zigzagging until he landed on his brood. His remaining escorts of two destroyers would not of course have been able to use their asdics, because at the speed required for landing on aircraft the asdic domes would have been raised. On balance, his decision was the only one that he could have made, and this was borne out by Commander (Air) Baker, whose job it was to advise the captain on such matters.

It can be seen that lack of training played a large part in the tragedy, and it is sad that it never really seems to come to light until it is too late. In wartime there is rarely any scope for 'on the job training'. Our adversaries learned that lesson long before we did.

Another factor that played a part in the sinking of *Courageous*, and indeed of many other ships in the early days of the war, was 'damage control'. The closing of X and Y watertight doors was always a factor in limiting the effect of flooding damage in any vessel, but it was not until 1940-41 that damage control became a subject in its own right to be taught in part one of the training of officers and ratings. It was only then included after costly losses in ships and men, and finally showed itself to be a subject that could no longer be neglected after the loss of *Ark Royal* in 1941 not far from Gibraltar. It will be remembered that the poor old *Ark* had been 'sunk' by Dr Goebbels' propaganda machine on many occasions prior to 1941, so it was not surprising that the nation was, to say the least, sceptical, when it was finally found to be true. The loss of *Ark Royal* was possibly due as much to lack of damage control as to enemy action. It was from that time that much greater emphasis was put on this very important subject, which later was to save many lives and ships. Even when it is obvious that the damage is fatal, the end can be postponed, giving more time to get men up from below and launch boats and other life-saving equipment. The Board of Inquiry remarked "Counter flooding recommendations C.P.1997(38) para 30 were not observed, and indeed not known by the officers."

It was remarked by many survivors that the sounding of the ship's siren not only made it almost impossible to hear any orders given, but added an eerie sense of drama to an already tense and frightening situation. One remarked, "It was as though the old girl knew that she was done for, and was protesting about the manner of her end."

The final irony is that earlier in the day on the 17th, Schuhart had decided that as he was running short of fuel he would end his operations that evening and return home. *If* only he had. If any one of these things had either not happened, or had happened in a different sequence or timescale, then things may have been different, but they didn't, and the lives of many men were lost and the lives of many others took an entirely different course.

The author now.

The author after joining the Royal Hospital School, aged eleven and eighteen.

Left to right: King George VI, Captain Makeig-Jones, Captain Lord Mountbatten. Fleet Revue in Weymouth Bay, early August, 1939.

Captain William Tofield Makeig-Jones, Royal Navy.
Born 1890, died 1939.

HMS *Courageous* in dry dock, stern on.

In happier days before the war. HMS *Courageous* with old Portsmouth to starboard, HMS *Dolphin* to port, Camper and Nicholson's boat yard on the bow.

Postcard in remembrance of the 518 men who drowned in the sinking of HMS *Courageous* in September 1939.

Postcard of an artist's impression of the sinking of HMS *Courageous*.

U29 which sank HMS *Courageous*.

Otto Schuhart of U29 speaks with Fritz Julius Lemp of U30 at Wilhelmshaven after the sinking of HMS *Courageous*.

A survivor leaving the Royal Naval Barracks.
One of the more fortunate ones.

Chapter Twelve
The Admiralty Regret

"The Admiralty regret to announce that the aircraft-carrier HMS *Courageous...*" Those words, which later in the war were to become so commonplace, struck my mother like a blow from a giant hand. She couldn't seem to comprehend it. I only partly understood, but could not seem to grasp the full implications. At eleven, it is asking a lot of a child to fully understand the implications of such a thing all at once. Mercifully, my seven-year-old brother grasped it to a lesser extent even than I did.

It was the Monday morning when this terrible news came through. The first reaction was stunned disbelief and after that, the sick feeling that it must be true. The days that followed were somewhat blurred, but there were some very vivid memories. The hours of waiting outside the gates of the Royal Naval Barracks, HMS *Drake*, where I had stood often waiting for my dad to come ashore, were punctuated by little bursts of activity, when survivors passed through, to the intense joy and relief of those who had waited for so long in hope, fear and prayer, and were at last rewarded.

I remember standing next to another lad, about my age; he too was with his mother and sister. We talked as boys will, and he said his dad was, if I remember rightly, a leading seaman. I rather too proudly announced that mine was a chief petty officer. I met him a couple of years ago in the course of my research and he reminded me that my mother berated me, saying, "It makes no difference, son – they are all the same." His father walked out of the barracks gate on that first day; mine never did. Death knows no rank. But as time passed along, and fewer came out, our hopes faded, and the icy shards of desolation chilled our hearts.

At the end of the second day, there were not so many now outside the gates, and each hour saw fewer. At last an old chief petty officer came out and passed among us. To my mother he said, "Go home, my love, you can't do any good here, there won't be any more tonight, they'll notify you if there is any news."

But there wasn't. The following day, Wednesday, at lunchtime there was a ring at the door. My mother answered, and I saw the expression of utter hopelessness on her face when she saw the telegram boy. She took the telegram from him as if it were tainted, slowly opened it, read it, and in a voice barely audible said, "There's no reply." She said nothing, but put her arms around both of us, and as the tears came, her heart broke. It read: "Deeply regret to report death of your husband CPO Cook Archibald H Gibbings 13161 on war service - Commodore Devonport." I still have that telegram, and even now when I look at it an icy hand grips me.

I have often contrasted those terrible wartime telegrams, curtly worded, with the way that people are notified under normal circumstances of the death of a dear one. But of course, in war it does not take long to grasp that all the niceties of life are among the first casualties.

When, at the end of July 1939, my father was recalled from pension, he realised that should war come there would be censorship. Being in a Devonport based ship, he knew that she would be in and out of Devonport more likely than not. He had warned my mother before leaving that should he advise her to do something she must read between the lines, and act on this advice.

While my father had been in the last year or two of his service, we had lived in the Camels Head district of Plymouth, about a mile from the naval barracks. We had a neighbour next door, Mrs Bell, with whom we kept in touch when we moved to London. It soon became obvious to Dad that *Courageous* was settling down to a pattern of anti-submarine patrols. Indeed the people of Cawsand, which looked out over the breakwater in Plymouth Sound, remarked about it and thought that for such a large ship to enter and leave harbour with such regularity was to invite trouble. However, mother had a letter from Dad in which he said, "As you and the boys haven't had a holiday this year, why don't you go and stay with Mrs Bell, I know she would be delighted." This we did, my mother leaving the next day. All the schools were closed indefinitely while the buildings were prepared for air raid precaution work, sand-bagging and window taping etc., so there was no problem in us children missing out in education. When we all arrived on Mrs Bell's doorstep, it was obvious that we were expected. My father went there every time he was ashore, and yes, he expected us.

This all happened at the beginning of the second week of the war. We saw my father that evening, and again on the evening of 15th September, and I remember walking down to the bus stop at the corner of Camels Head School and seeing him standing on the platform of the bus and waving to us all the way along Wolseley Road… That was the last time I ever saw him. The picture of Dad, waving to us as he went was the one which I will remember most of him; forty-eight hours later he was gone.

Having seen him so recently made the shock of losing him more difficult to cope with. We just could not grasp the fact that he would never walk through the door again, his lovely old face smiling. I don't think that I ever saw his face without the threat of a smile bursting through at any moment.

I once heard a radio programme in which it was said that there were more attempted prison camp escapes made by RAF aircrew than other servicemen. It was suggested that this was due to the fact that most of them were captured after being shot down only, in some cases, an hour or two after leaving home, and in some cases even perhaps having breakfasted with wives or mothers. The shock of being "in the bag", perhaps for many years, so soon after leaving loved ones, was so great that they couldn't accept the situation and attempted escape as soon after as possible. Whereas, in the case of men who had been away from their families for months or even years, the sudden shock was not there, and no such mental rebellion against such a situation existed. However, I only know that I just could not come to terms with the sudden loss, and even now have never really come to terms with it.

For days we lived in a twilight world, half alive and only slightly aware of the world around us. One thing that I became aware of very quickly was that my world would never be the same again. I was nearly two months from my eleventh birthday when *Courageous* sank, and my brother just past seven. I have often thought that it was perhaps a little less sharp for him. It is difficult at that age to grasp the full implications of what had happened. He knew that something was wrong, but quite what it was he couldn't make out. Because of this I think it dawned on him over a period of days and weeks.

It would perhaps have been better if the schools had been open, but they weren't, and we had nothing to do but think, and being in Plymouth away from our playmates in London we were thrown back on our own resources, which at that time were scanty. There was at that time a great deal of sympathy, for it was so early in the war and it was the first great tragedy, with many more to come. As one survivor said, *Courageous* was not the only ship to go, merely the first, so in that respect we were perhaps more fortunate than those who lost relatives later. It was not to be long before the death of loved ones was so commonplace that it scarcely evoked more than a momentary expression of regret; an offer of sympathy and help, and a feeling in the person that offered, that while they were genuinely sorry, you were one of tens of thousands. There was a war on, and this sort of thing happens. It could be me next time.

The first few days I filled my time by watching the son of one of my father's friends, a man he had known in the service. He was a boot and shoe repairer and ran his business in a shed at the bottom of his garden. I asked lots of questions which of course he could not answer, and which I now realise made him feel uncomfortable. He was very patient, but I now realise just how relieved he must have been when I finally gave up and went away.

It was then that the worst period in my mother's life began. She had no brothers or sisters and her father had died when she was eleven and her mother just after her twenty-first birthday.

Up to the time of Dad's recall from pension we had lived an idyllic life in the London suburb of Queensbury. Our lifestyle was good; not luxurious, but very comfortable. Dad had his naval pension, and had taken up his new job in the General Post Office as a civil servant. We were buying our house, and had made a start on the very large garden. It was the end house in a long road and was going to need a good deal of work, but listening to him and Mum planning, it was going to be a labour of love, and they joked about being Mr and Mrs Suburbia; I had never known them happier.

The morning that we left 179 Turner Road, Queensbury, I never dreamed that I would never return there to live. My brother and I had attended Stag Lane School, which, when we went to that district in 1937, was ultra-modern. I loved it from the start, and can never remember being so happy at school. Unlike all the other schools I had attended up till then, I never saw a cane used, and seldom a hard word. The winter of 1938 was very cold, and I remember it snowing, and catching a chill. I had always had a chest weakness and asthma, and the chill quickly progressed to a very serious pneumonia and I was carted off to hospital. I remember very little except waking up from a delirious sleep and trying to get a drink from the bathroom tap. My father, hearing me, and going into the bathroom, found me on the floor. I was scarcely conscious during the drive to hospital and remained in that twilight zone for several days with, I learned later, a temperature nearing a 105°.

The three weeks I remained in hospital spanned Christmas 1938, and so I missed being with my father during the last Christmas of his life.

When I returned to school, it surprised me that I was treated by the other children as if I was just back from the dead. It appeared that our class teacher, Mr Edmonds, had been taken away at the same time as me and had died of pneumonia. I don't think there was a child in that class not affected by his death. He was an excellent pianist and gave me my first interest in classical music with one of Handel's pieces from *Berenice*. He was a really gentle young man; a little pale with fair thinning hair and a small moustache to match, and as I remember a wan expression hinting at sadness. He was missed by the whole class, and yes, well-loved. It was a lovely school, with excellent teachers, to whom I shall always be grateful. Mr King the headmaster, a man whose dark moustache and sombre appearance belied his true gentle, kindly nature; Miss Pitts, later Mrs Carpenter, a very accomplished pianist, and a most attractive lady. Then there was Mr Gray, a young smartly dressed man with an easy manner, and Mr Cutts, a shortish rotund man whose visage seemed at first a little severe, but whose smile was not far away, even in admonishment. The last, Mrs Lambert, only taught me for a week or two. She was a little more strict, and the lessons lacked that little bit of levity which endeared the others to me, nevertheless, she wasn't unkind, but had her own ways of getting results. Finally, Mr Stacey, a tall smart man of early middle age. He was never one of my class teachers, but taught the violin. The school had a scheme which enabled those whose parents could afford it to purchase a violin for six pence a week, and have lessons for three pence. I was fortunate in that my parents could afford this, and thereby began a lifelong love of music, and although I never attained great distinction, it is a thing that I treasure and thank both Mr Edmonds and Mr Stacey for. Yes, Stag Lane was a happy school, and one that I knew I would enjoy when I first approached it with my father to enrol. I can remember the enthusiastic singing of "Cherry Ripe" as I approached, and when days later I attended morning assembly, singing some of the hymns I love best, "Loving Shepherd of thy sheep", "When morning gilds the skies", "The King of love my Shepherd is". These and many others were sung enthusiastically by all of us, and I am certain that many of us enjoyed these early morning assemblies; I certainly did, but sadly now they are becoming a thing of the past. Yes, I have a lot to thank Stag Lane School for. It was a great source of grief to me that I never went back there as a pupil after my father's death, although I did visit it a year or so later when a pupil of the Royal Hospital School, and often think of the sharp contrast.

In the days that followed, my mother's unaided task was to close the door on the happiest part of her life, and open the door into a future that lay along a path beset with worry, anxiety, and the hardship of war. First she had to return to London and settle the family's affairs. My brother stayed with Mrs Bell in Plymouth, and I spent the next few weeks with an aunt; one of my father's sisters, in Newton Abbot. I cannot answer for my brother, but I know that on top of losing Dad, there was always the awful fear of losing Mum too, and although my aunt was good to me, I felt this awful longing to be with Mum again.

There was first of all my father's life insurance. His life was well insured for an amount that should have covered the cost of the house, but... there was a clause in the policy which stated that if the insured was killed by act of war etc., etc., there would only be a return of the premiums unless an additional war risk premium was paid. The war was but two weeks old, and the insurance company couldn't, of course, explain how a man who had been called back into the Navy and had been at sea since the outbreak of war could possibly be expected to pay the war risk premium, even if he had been reminded of this particular clause by the company, which of course he had not. Legally, they were within their rights; morally they could not have been more wrong. Their flat refusal to honour such a moral obligation was despicable. In these times I do not believe that any company would be allowed to get away with such practice, but I know the effect of this body blow on my dear mother. It affected our lives permanently, indeed our lives took a completely different turn, and we followed a new path.

The next thing she had to do was give up the house that we had come to love after less than two happy years. There was no way that she could cope with a mortgage on her greatly reduced income, a drop from over six pounds a week to one pound seventeen shillings and six pence. There was only one way out for her. She had to leave the house, and walk out. The only concession being that the mortgage payments already made would be accepted as rent for the period that we had occupied it.

Mum accepted this and came back to Plymouth, taking a tiny flat in York Road, Camels Head. This in itself must have been torture, being so near to the rented house we occupied just before my father pensioned from the service; the place of so many of their dreams and hopes.

The first Christmas was for us children quite pleasant, apart from the fact that every now and then little thoughts of Christmas past would creep in and torture us. There were many moments when my mother was near despair. It was many years before I fully realised just how deep was her pain and anguish.

I have to say that the first Christmas for us children was not too hard. We lacked nothing. We had presents from a fund provided by an Indian Rajah, and very nice presents they were. There was also a bag of coal from our local church, St Philip's at Camels Head. The vicar at that time was the Reverend Prebendary Jesse Brown, a real Christian gentleman, and the gift was typical, and practical, as was his gift to me personally – the offer to be one of his choirboys. My voice was not all that good, but neither was it bad, and I can truly say that I did enter into the spirit of the thing, and was at least enthusiastic, but leaving out all pretence to the niceties.

I still feel that the Reverend Brown only offered me a place in the choir in order that I would have a little pocket-money like the other lads. I would like to have had the opportunity to have repaid his kindness, but he has passed on to his reward. He did quite a lot for young people, including being the chaplain to the local Air Training Corps, and I am sure that he earned his place in heaven. For many years he remained the vicar of St Philip's, and fulfilled his duties with the aid of his old Austin Ruby car. He always reminded me of Friar Tuck, and I can to this day picture him in his cassock driving his old car. The two of them were well-suited - unostentatious, reliable, and redolent of a better age of good practical Christianity. Our first Christmas without Dad was made a little more bearable by this lovely old man.

Chapter Thirteen
Of Naval Uncles

I have until now dealt with the cold facts of the sinking of *Courageous*, and followed with a brief account of the early days after, and tried as far as possible to convey the utter desolation, and shock which we suffered. But the story really goes back further than that. I have not, until now, said anything of naval uncles. Now, I don't know whether or not any other children had them, but I did. At least I had two. My brother only had one because my first naval uncle came into our lives a little before he was born.

I have already said that the Navy was a great big family, and that men still at home would keep an eye on the families of old shipmates and friends. Well we, like many others, experienced this system of unofficial social work, for that is what it was. It was something that cannot be related to the present because the times were different, and so were the people. There were two families in particular that I remember with great affection. The first was Whitehead, at least that was how I knew him. I don't remember now what he looked like because I was only a baby at the time. That may seem strange, but I am gifted with a memory that goes back to when I was eighteen months old. I cannot remember a great many things of that time but I distinctly remember that I was having a great deal of trouble in cutting teeth, and this caused both my mother and me many sleepless nights. However, I solved the problem for myself. One day when my mother was shopping, and Whitehead was looking after me as he often did, I made a grab at one of his pipes lying on the table, and started gnawing at it. Each time he took it away from me I howled, but while I gnawed at it I was quite contented. Eventually, he cleaned out and boiled one of his old pipes and gave it to me. That was the end of all my teething troubles, and probably the reason that I smoked a pipe for many years until I had the good sense to kick the tobacco habit in my mid-fifties.

I spent many hours with Whitehead, happy hours. Like most navy men he could be stern, but always, underneath, the kind word and smile was never far away. He was my first naval uncle, and I remember him still although he is gone. He was killed not long after my father, on 23rd November 1939, when the armed merchant cruiser HMS *Rawalpindi*, on patrol between the Faeroes and Iceland, met up with the Scharnhorst and Gneisenau. She was outgunned, outranged, and no match for the enemy; an ex-P & O liner of 17,000 tons with a few 6" popguns, against two battleships of 34,000 tons, each carrying nine 11" and twelve 5.9" guns. *Rawalpindi* was doomed from the start. There were only thirty-seven survivors. It was ironic that the captain of the *Rawalpindi*, Captain Edward Coverley Kennedy, should go down with his ship, because he had been a victim of Geddes' axe (1923), that criminally stupid piece of legislation which removed from the service so many of our most experienced officers, only to recall them when it was too late. This was a piece of folly from which we have learned nothing, and we are being treated to a repeat performance. Let us hope that it does not result in the death of as many of our servicemen as it did last time. I witnessed the effect first hand. Whitehead's widow Peggy and my mother worked together at the Royal Naval Armament Depot in Plymouth all through the war, partly because each of them had two young children and could not possibly afford even the basic essentials on the appallingly low level of war widows and orphans pension. I witnessed their tears of grief and despair more than once, and will not forget.

My other naval uncle was Uncle Bill. Bill Hillson. I had known him since, I think, 1934, when my parents occupied the upstairs flat of a lovely house at Milne Villas, opposite the Portland Road gate of Devonport Park. This was the happiest time of our life prior to our short sojourn in London. Uncle Bill, with his wife Aunty Edith, and their two daughters, Lena and Doris, lived in the flat below. At the time of our moving in there, my father was about half way through a two-and-a-half-year commission in the China fleet. This was the second move my mother had made on her own since my father had been away.

Uncle Bill was a master-at-arms, the regulating or police branch of the service. He was of medium height and, although certainly not fat, was rotund. His face was round, open and pleasant, but if you overstepped the mark, one glance would immediately let you know. He was like most of the navy men I knew; good with kids, and always had that twinkle of fun in his eye. We were there until shortly before my father left the service on pension, and many were the kindnesses that we were shown by this lovely couple while Dad was away, particularly when one of us children was ill or out of sorts. I am sure that the only fault that they had was to spoil us. When we left Milne Villas, little did we know that the next time we saw Uncle Bill and Aunty Edith, it was going to be well over three years later, and under such different circumstances.

The war had started; *Courageous* had been sunk, and Dad had gone. Uncle Bill was in the RN Barracks and had learned of our loss. I remember well the first time that Mum took us boys to their home after. They both openly wept, and their grief was genuine. But being the people that they were, their help was of a practical nature. Every Friday evening, Mum took us two boys to tea with them, and she and Aunty Edith would sit and talk, while Uncle Bill would play Ludo with my brother and me. Early in 1940, I started asking about going to a naval school, the Royal Hospital School. This was the start of a different life for me.

As if it was not enough for us to have experienced already what a war was really like, we had more to come, but this time we were not alone. It was one Friday evening, some time after I had started my new life and I was on leave from the naval school, that we were spending the evening at Uncle Bill's home, which was in a little street adjacent to the RN Engineering College, HMS *Thunderer*. We had just left to take the bus home to St Budeaux, and the air raid warning sounded. I remember that this was the early days of the Plymouth blitz. We waited at the bus stop, hoping that a bus would come along and pick us up if only to take us away from the dockyard and naval barracks area, which was of course what the bombers were after. Several buses did come along, but none stopped. We later learned that in the event of an air raid, they had instructions to return to the depot without stopping. Realising that the worst thing that we could do was to stay where we were, we started to walk towards St Budeaux. We heard the first warning shots of the anti-aircraft guns as we started to walk, and the rate of fire increased as we reached St Levan's gate. My young brother and I were terrified as the bombs had started to fall. We kept going along the high dockyard wall, feeling that it might afford us some shelter from the shrapnel, which, by now was falling around us. The strange thing was that we were the only living creatures passing along that road, and we didn't see a soul until we came to the gates of HMS *Drake*, the Royal Naval Barracks. There was a sentry standing just within the gate, with a Royal Marine policeman. My mother asked the policeman if there was anywhere we could shelter. I can see him now. It was obvious that he was sympathetic, but there was nothing that he could do. He asked how far we had to go, and when we told him he advised us that the best thing to do was to keep going, but avoid the short cut to St Budeaux across "Shaky bridge". The road to St Budeaux added a mile to our journey as it formed a sort of horseshoe, with the bridge spanning the two ends of the horseshoe; but it lay right alongside the naval base, and that was what the bombers were after. We eventually got home, but I can never remember a more terrifying journey - one which I never thought that we would complete alive. We learned next morning that Boscawen block in the barracks had been hit with very great loss of life. I will never forget the noise and the smell of smoke, and the tinkle of shrapnel as it fell. Once again, what were my mother's thoughts in the middle of all that hell, I wonder. I only know that her courage, although she was undoubtedly frightened for us, never left her.

We were amongst the first to experience the grief and loss that is war, but this was our very first taste of the gut-twisting fear of being killed or maimed. Like many others, we went through more as time went by, but although one never really gets used to it, it is like any wound, it forms scar tissue which although it leaves a permanent mark, does tend to inure one against future similar experiences.

From the earliest part of my life that I can remember, I had always wanted to join the Royal Navy. There was never any question of becoming a fireman, train driver, or a policeman; only the Navy would do, and I wanted to join as soon as I could, but, at the age of eleven, it would be some years before I could even join as a boy. The nearest that I could get to joining the Navy at that age was to enter the Royal Hospital School. This was a school for the sons of serving and past members of the Royal Navy, Royal Marines, the Merchant Service, Trinity House, and bona fide fishing fleets. Preference was given to orphans, and during the war the school was filled to capacity.

In return for educating them, the boys were expected to enter the Royal Navy on completion of their time at the school. So, at fifteen years of age, boys who were not medically fit would be found employment in civilian life, very often in the naval dockyards and ordnance factories, etc., but if they passed, they would remain and complete another year, and then go on to HMS *Ganges* or one of the many other boys' training establishments. It will be seen that this was a very lucrative source of recruitment for the service. All the boys entering the service from the school already had a very thorough grounding in discipline and naval routine, and the discipline of the Navy was certainly no shock to their system as it often was to those who had not had the benefit of such an education.

My mother, to say the least, was not very keen on the idea. My health had never been too good. Less than a year before, I had nearly succumbed to pneumonia, and had suffered from asthma all my life, and had spent a year in a sanatorium. It is hardly surprising that she was concerned. But my mind was made up. The following Friday when we went to Uncle Bill's for the evening, my mother asked him to have a word with me and explain the full implications of entering into such a hard life. For hard it was, and once you were there you were committed. It was wartime Britain, and life was serious, and nobody had the time or inclination to cope with people who couldn't make up their mind what they wanted. Uncle Bill took great pains to tell me about life in the school, and that you would be subjected to strict naval discipline and could not go home in the evening and tell your mum if you were not happy, and that boys there were caned for what might seem to be very minor offences. I was not to be deflected from my purpose, and Uncle Bill sent for the papers. Within a few weeks I was accepted and became a pupil of the Royal Hospital School.

If ever I had thought that life there was not going to be so strict as he had painted it, then I soon altered my ideas. Every minute of the day was all activity. Up early to make your own beds, darn your own socks, cleaning stations, assembly, square-bashing, sports, classes in all subjects including religious instruction, seamanship, signals, woodwork, and a host of other things. Life was never the same again.

Did I have any regrets? Yes, in the early days, quite a lot. To come from a very loving and protective environment, where all my needs were catered for, my shoes cleaned, my socks darned, my vest warmed and ready after a bath, and nearly all my thinking done for me, and to be suddenly plunged into what was without any doubt a service environment, at the tender age of eleven, is, to say the least, a severe jolt to the whole system. It was a shock to the seventeen-year-old who found himself suddenly catapulted into the services, so you can imagine what it was like for a mere child, for that is what we were. Many a lad cried himself to sleep for weeks after his arrival there, but before too long you realised that you had to get on with it, and Mum couldn't help you anymore. But having said that, there is no question in my mind that it did equip us for the life we were about to lead, or indeed for any future. It taught self-reliance, and an ability to live and work with all types of people, and to accept them for what they were. It taught you to pull your weight and not to expect others to wait on you, and it taught you team spirit and loyalty to your country, the service, your ship and each other. Yes, the school gave me a lot; I didn't realise it at the time, or for some time after, but later I found that the many habits and ways that it had indelibly printed in my mind stood me in good stead, and I am grateful.

Uncle Bill and Aunty Edith are both gone now, but I can still see them both - good, solid, lovely people of a bygone age who unstintingly helped our little family with advice and encouragement at a time that we needed it most. It was only two years later that Uncle Bill came near to losing his life, when on 10th December 1941, the battleship HMS *Prince of Wales* on which he was serving was sunk in the South China sea, in the company of the battle cruiser HMS *Repulse*, with horrendous loss of life. Even worse was to come. Many of the survivors were sent up country to assist the army in a vain attempt to stem the rapid advance of the Japanese army. This resulted in their capture and internment in Japanese prison camps, which many of them did not survive. Thankfully, Uncle Bill was one of the more fortunate, in that he was returned home. But I am sure that this episode of his life, and the loss of so many of his shipmates and friends, left scars that he took to his grave.

I count myself very fortunate in having known men like Whitehead and Bill Hillson. Indeed, the Navy at that time seemed to have a mould that produced them. In the course of my research, I received a letter from a retired Lt.-Cdr. David Roberts RN, who knew two of the men who lost their lives in *Courageous*, and sent me an account of their story. I asked his permission to include this as he had written it, which he kindly gave me. He knew these two men, as I did Uncle Bill and Whitehead, and was obviously very moved and upset at their passing. I may be wrong, but I cannot remember many men, in the last thirty years at least, with the qualities of these. And sadly, I do not think on today's showing that I will meet many more.

Chapter Fourteen

Chief Petty Officer A. Lumber

– Torpedo Gunner's Mate
HMS *Courageous* – September 1939

by Lt.-Cdr. D. Roberts RN Rtd

Many of us who belonged to the old fraternity of the Torpedo Branch in the Devonport Division remember the three old hulks, *Vulcan*, *Inconstant* and *Andromeda*, tied up together at Wilcove near Torpoint, known collectively as HMS *Defiance*, the Torpedo and Electrical School for the West Country Division until the end of World War II. There was no separate Electrical Department as known today: the Torpedo Department, like the Gunnery Department, was 'Seaman first'. In a sense it was a small community and although facilities were poor and cramped, it produced men of the highest calibre, possessing a personal and professional pride in their department and the service as a whole. Naturally, everyone knew each other, their background, character and their worth. Even now, when some fifty years have rolled by since the end of World War II, those men still stand out in my mind as rough-hewn characters, each an individual in his own right, all sorts and types, but sharing an unshakeable faith in the Navy, for such were the men of the King's Navy. I often look back over the gruelling and perilous war years. Many of our ships were obsolete and leftovers from the First World War, and at times we had our limitations and grievous material shortcomings, but what distinguished the British Navy was that it was always at sea – everywhere at all times and under all conditions – but I digress.

My first recollections of then Petty Officer Lumber (TGM) would be in the latter thirties both at *Defiance* and at Malta, when we were serving in the Mediterranean Fleet. He was the TI of the submarine

'Snapper'. He was a chap who got about and he had a habit of appearing at some unexpected place at some unexpected time. Over those few years up to 1939 I came to know him as a good friend, a friend among his many friends, attracted by his frank, cheerful and wholesome nature. In a way he was a breezy character with a loud and infectious laugh and he loved company. You felt that he had a personal interest in your well-being.

In the days before the war, promotion was exceedingly slow. It was very much a long serviceman's navy, therefore Albert Lumber was exceptional since he was a petty officer with a first class rate – TGM in his first period of service – twelve years. He was highly recommended and urged to go through for warrant officer – gunner (T) – but he refused to do so as he considered that he would lose contact with the men, bearing in mind that in those days it was a socially rigid navy with little communication between the ranks. I have heard many speak of him but always with esteem and respect. As an individual he was of medium build but well-rounded, with a fresh complexion. His manner was direct and he both looked at you and through you at the same time. He was a natural leader who could take people with him. He had a sad marriage in so far as I can remember him saying, as his wife died early in marriage, leaving him a daughter. I believe she lived in Bristol.

Above all else he was a dedicated Christian, to whom his Christian calling was expressed in service to his fellows; in this he was something of a human dynamo, always helping somebody some way or other before thinking of himself. The Navy then was highly disciplined, and autocratically officered; welfare was hardly known and men spent long periods at sea away from their homes and families with little leave. A foreign commission was two-and-a-half years long, quite often soon followed by another. In those days when a ship commissioned, the whole ship's company marched to their ship from the barracks, headed by the Royal Marine band, and so it was that for the next two-and-a-half years you looked at the same faces across the mess table. The strain on sailors was immense, some with feckless wives and others with large families whom they longed to see. Pay was poor for the lower rates. Many had difficult problems which they bore alone and without complaint.

It was about July 1939 when my ship *Norfolk* was in dockyard hands in Devonport undergoing a major refit, being practically gutted with turbines and shafts on shore, when it so happened that I met Albert Lumber. He asked me if I wanted to take over his little bed-sitting room which he rented, as he intended to move to more commodious accommodation in the Royal Sailors' Rest in Fore Street. This I did with great alacrity. The landlady was a kindly and rather elderly little lady, Miss Pym, who produced remarkably good meals using only a small oil stove. Although it was modest accommodation I thought it was marvellous, as it was somewhere to go away from the ship wallowing in the dockyard discomfort. Albert had left the digs but he told me that he would collect a suit sometime as he had forgotten to take it with him. So it was on a Saturday afternoon in August that he turned up.

At the time I was studying for a GPO exam in telephony which I hoped to take on leaving the service the following year (1940) when I was due to finish my period of seven years (short service). That particular day, I remember, I had little heart in what I was doing. Somehow, there was a sense of uncertainty and a feeling that war with Germany was not far off. The weather was hot and heavy, so it was good to stop and have a chat over a pot of tea provided by Miss Pym. Albert was good company and his usual warm and cheerful self. To my great pleasure he was now wearing a chief petty officer's uniform and he told me that he was now on the aircraft-carrier *Courageous*. He spoke with great pride and affection of the Torpedo Division of which he was the regulating chief petty officer, the total staff being about sixty-two. Also on board there was a Petty Officer (TGM) Harry Shore, a very active Christian man, whom he knew very well. The conversation drifted to that which was uppermost in our minds – not so much *if* there would be a war but *when*. We both had the feeling that Britain was becoming engulfed in something intensely evil; one could almost hear the stamp of the German jackboot. Anyway, the time soon came for Albert to go as he was a very busy man, at times he seemed to work himself to exhaustion. He then asked for his suit. I remember looking at it hanging behind the door and as I lifted it down I was surprised to see that the material was exactly like that of my own suit hanging underneath it. I hadn't noticed this before, so I held up both suits to see which was which. "This one is yours," I said to Albert and I replaced mine. As I passed him his I said involuntarily and without thinking, "One taken and one left". As he took it I noticed that tears were dropping down his cheeks. In a way I was taken by surprise, even more so when I realised that his concern was not for himself but for me. I didn't think that he cared so much. He then departed and that was to be the last occasion I was to see him.

Events moved very quickly. Leave became restricted and I had to give up my little 'bedsitter', having hardly moved in. My ship crawled with 'Dockyardies', her shafts and engines almost jumped back into her, never had there been so much activity in the dockyard in living memory. Soon *Norfolk* was back in one piece, steam was raised and she proceeded to sea for trials, completing them in the first days of September. I remember the evening of 2nd September 1939, when the ship had returned from sea and anchored inside the breakwater of Plymouth Sound. It was a warm, clear and beautiful evening and I was taking my evening stroll up and down the four-inch gun deck, when I happened to look towards the breakwater. There was *Courageous* anchored close by, and a huge harvest moon seemed to be resting on the flight deck.

A few hours later *Norfolk* left at high speed and on the following day when in St George's Channel I heard the fateful news over the loudspeaker in my mess that Britain was now at war. Nobody had much to say but we all wondered what lay before us and one thing was certain that when it was all over nothing would ever be the same again. Shortly afterwards, our thirty-two knot cruiser signalled that seventeen knots maximum could only be maintained at great hazard due to engine trouble. *Norfolk* proceeded to Scapa Flow and then on to her Arctic war station patrolling the Denmark Straits (which separated Iceland and Greenland) and towards Jan Mayen Island. *Hood* and *Suffolk* were in the same area.

My job was searchlight LTO and my station was on the port and starboard searchlights situated on connecting platforms halfway up the after funnel. RDF – later known as radar – was not then fitted in *Norfolk*, so target contact at night was made by starshell and searchlight. I was on my own, the nights were long, the position very exposed.

In the early months of the war rumour was rife and facts few because of security reasons and we were out of contact with true events being far north. 'Lord Haw-Haw' on the German radio had 'sunk' practically every ship in the British Navy including our own, but the rumour of the loss of the *Courageous* persisted and I began to fear for Albert Lumber's safety.

The regulating chief petty officer (TGM) of *Norfolk* was CPO 'Knocker' White, a shortish upright Scot from Greenock. He was a fine man indeed, highly efficient, forthright and straight in his dealings, a strict disciplinarian but very human. He was held in high esteem by all and he inspired confidence in the staff.

On one particular night, when the ship was far north and the nights were becoming very cold, but before the time when the harsh weather set in and the ship turned to a solid block of rock ice on the upper decks, I had just been relieved from my watch on the searchlights and was making my way down to my mess by my usual route. This took me down the central hatch leading from the upper deck by the torpedo tubes, through the canteen flat, along the main deck to my mess situated abreast 'A' turret. It gave me some pleasure to feel the warmth from the boiler and engine rooms and see lights and people after my lonely watch. As I was passing the torpedo regulating office on my way, the brown curtain which covered the open door was swept aside and CPO White stepped out in front of me. It is strange how you remember little things – I noticed that other than his usual immaculate appearance his shoe laces were missing. Obviously he had something on his mind which he intended to say to me. He spoke as if he was giving way to pent-up feelings and he said almost with vehemence "I talked to... [I can't remember his name, but I didn't know him anyway, but he was a survivor from *Courageous* who was about the last person to see Albert Lumber alive.] According to him, he could have saved himself quite easily but he held back to help a group of non-swimmers. As he was struggling to launch a boat time ran out, *Courageous* heeled, the seas broke in and she went down." 'Knocker' White then paused and said with great feeling, "He died as he lived – helping others – he could easily have saved himself." I didn't say anything, somehow I seemed to have known already that Albert Lumber had gone down with his ship. I resumed my walk forward to my mess deck with a feeling of desolation. So this is war – what madness – what waste!

Although this incident happened when the ship had been at sea for some days, I concluded that CPO White must have talked to someone he knew in the canteen at Scapa Flow. The following year CPO White and myself left *Norfolk* and returned to HMS *Defiance* for promotion courses. CPO White was promoted to warrant rank, gunner (T), meanwhile I qualified torpedo gunner's mate (TGM) as a leading seaman, passed for petty officer. We both went to destroyers and eighteen months later I returned to *Defiance* to qualify warrant officer, gunner (T), joining another destroyer on promotion. During that period at *Defiance* I heard that Mr White, gunner (T) RN, had gone down with his ship while on convoy duties.

Some years later, after the war I had a poignant reminder of the tragedy of war. I was reintroduced to Mrs Harry Shore, the wife of Harry Shore of *Courageous*. I remembered her as a young wife in 1939 and now I could not recognise the elderly looking lady before me. Very recently she died. She had kept all the clothes and belongings of her husband who had died with Albert Lumber in the *Courageous*. I was told that she would not believe that her husband had gone down in *Courageous* but that he had been picked up by a passing ship and someday would return when he would need his clothes. The years passed but he never returned.

At the onset of war we were ill prepared. At first it seemed that the nation was reluctant to accept that it was at war. We were only just beginning to drag ourselves out of the terrible economic depression of the thirties. In contrast, Germany's war machine was superbly trained and equipped, ready and poised to strike. From the very start the Royal and Merchant Navies were very much at war and suffered grievous losses. For many it was a long war, first we had to learn to fight and survive and then, to win. But war is sad and life the cheapest commodity. To me Albert Lumber became a sort of reference point where human values mattered, the shining example in a disintegrating and perilous world.

Chapter Fifteen
Devonport

Devonport was a naval town. I say that because at one time its mainstay was the Navy and the naval dockyard, and most of its economy was geared to the service and its needs. The military also played a very large part in Devonport's everyday life and commerce, but it was primarily the Navy which provided the bread and butter for the majority of families.

I remember when the home fleet came in after a summer cruise or exercise, that Albert Road and William Street would be packed with sailors that weekend. Looking up Albert Road and along William Street on a Saturday night one would see navy blue uniforms the whole length of both streets, and hear the hubbub coming from the doorways of the many pubs and eating places. Unlike today, those two streets, consisting of small shops, naval tailors, tobacconists, barbers and the like, derived their living from the service and their families. Indeed it would not be unfair to say, that for its size, Devonport was a far more vital and pulsating community than Plymouth.

My parents lived at Keyham when I was born, but moved to Millbridge not long after, and occupied rooms over a shop on Eldad Hill. I well remember the two big events of my day when I was only three years old. At that time most of the transport of heavy objects and machinery in the dockyard was carried out by horses, and these were supplied by a civilian firm that stabled the horses at Millbay. Every evening, I would take up my position in the upstairs room which commanded a view of the whole road from corner to corner, and wait. Eventually these lovely great beasts would come around the corner from the Victoria Park end and clip-clop up the hill, one man in front and another at the rear. I loved this evening ritual, which I called 'The string of Gee-Gees', and it was the highlight of my day.

The other thing that I wouldn't miss was the lamplighter. He came around at dusk with his long pole, lit the gas flame, and was gone. It was over in a few seconds, but I wouldn't miss it for the world.

The early thirties were fairly happy times for my parents and in Devonport, although wages were very low, there was an attitude in the community that encouraged people to help themselves and rely on each other. In 1932, my father was drafted to a destroyer on the China station, HMS *Witch*, and I remember that I was most upset at his going away, and my most vivid memory is of seeing him waving from the observation platform of the Southern Railway train taking him to Portsmouth to embark in the ship which was to take him away. It seems ironic that history repeated itself seven years later, when my last sight of my father was as he stood on the platform of a bus waving to us for what was to be the last time... only two days before he was killed.

Almost as soon as he was gone, Mother, now three months pregnant with my brother, moved from our flat at Eldad Hill to rooms on the top floor above the Lord Beresford public house in Cumberland Street Devonport. The landlady of the pub was a Mrs Gill whose husband was, like my father, a petty officer, and an old shipmate. It was there that my brother was born, while Mrs Gill looked after me downstairs. In those times this was a commonplace occurrence; home confinements were the norm, and there was certainly little or no welfare support. It is strange that little things tend to remind one of such events; that was the day that I lost my one-eyed teddy bear. I never saw him again!! I remember Devonport as a place of kindly neighbours and characters.

It must be remembered that at that time it was not unusual for a foreign commission to keep a man away from his family for two-and-a-half years, indeed that was the usual period of time that he was away. Sometimes it could be as long as three years. There was little or no welfare to help them as there is today, only their own inner strength and resilience came to their aid, and they had it aplenty. Unlike today, divorce was unheard of, there was no welfare state, and mothers didn't go crying to the social services.

It is said that we don't remember days: we remember moments. This is true in the context that we don't remember every moment of any day, but just the highlights which are connected by hazy memories of the general tenor and influence of that particular day. The same applies to both good and bad memories.

At this time one of the highlights of our life were my father's frequent letters. When I say frequent, I must add that it took weeks for them to reach us, but once a ship arrived on station the letters started to flow and were always numbered. My father's letters were always very interesting, and my mother would read them to me in bed; I was too young for school then, but Dad used to write a special letter for me, and a drawing, always a drawing of a group of Ooslum birds. They looked something like ostriches and lived on a diet of whalebone corsets and rusty bedsteads, and had a nasty habit of writing letters to Dad informing him of any breaches of good behaviour!

Those days have always stuck in my mind as being very special, and I particularly remember the safe feeling I always had. Although both Mum and Dad came from Dawlish, Mum had no parents alive and no brothers or sisters. Dad had some family still there, but none anywhere near, yet, although there was only the four of us, we felt like a real family, safe, warm and secure, no thought ever of our family breaking up. Certainly not for the reasons that families break up today. Mum was always there to warm us when we were cold, and nurse us when we were sick and tempt us with food when we were getting better. I still think of it as a cocoon of warmth, and despite one member of the family being away a lot, he still seemed to be around in a strange sort of way, and was spoken of every day as if he would come in at any time. Even years later when Dad was killed, Mother still managed to maintain the unity of our little family. How very fortunate I have been in having such parents.

But we all have many memories that seem to stay with us and tend not to fade, and I know that I shall retain very happy recollections of that time. It was the Navy, with help from the army, that made Devonport and Plymouth so cosmopolitan. So many servicemen stationed here met, courted and married local girls, and the majority settled here permanently after marriage and even after leaving the service. The biggest employers were the Navy and the dockyard, and many thousands got their living from both of these. Trade and commerce thrived in Devonport between the wars, and although even in those days the pay was very meagre, the people of Devonport somehow made ends meet, and I never experienced anyone going hungry. Even those at the bottom of the heap were somehow looked after even if only by the generosity of those a little better off. There was a spirit abroad in those days that made Devonport a good place to live in. I was a Devonport boy and have always been proud of it, and although it has altered in so many ways I can still see it as it was, and to me Devonport was the Navy, and the Navy was Devonport. They were inextricably tied to each other, and all other employment and commerce was tied to them in so many ways.

From Cumberland Street we moved to Milne Villas, a flat above another naval family, the Hillsons, Uncle Bill. It was almost opposite the Portland Road entrance to Devonport Park; in my opinion the loveliest of Plymouth's parks. Devonport Park was where my mother took my brother and I on every day that the weather allowed. It was frequented by so many naval wives and families whose men were away at sea, but I can never remember any moaning or carping about the very poor pay and conditions suffered by the men and their wives at that time, at least in comparison to their present day counterparts. Rather the talk was of their men and when they would be home again, their children and schools, and how best to make their money stretch, and what current prices were at Devonport market and the shops in Albert Road.

I well remember the lovely old bandstand in the park where a number of regimental and Royal Marine bands played at the weekends, one of the free pleasures all the locals could enjoy. The attractive old lodge where teas were served, with its ornate cast iron balcony, I can still see, but I never remember going inside it. It is now an old people's home and still retains much of its old-world charm. I can never go in that park now without remembering it as it *was* in those days, and the happy hours I spent there, but sadly now the park has been cut in two. This was done many years ago now after the decision to kill off Devonport was taken. Although this was never admitted, it was effectively killed off in order to justify the rebuilding of Plymouth City Centre.

I can never understand why it was necessary to take such a large slice of Devonport into dockyard use at a time when the Navy was in decline and less work was being done in the dockyard. The whole of the area around the market and west of Chapel Street, and the whole of Fore Street was taken. William Street was closed and only New Passage Hill and Marlborough Street remained. The new road, Park

Avenue, ran from Albert Road across the park to what was left of Fore Street, and from there down Chapel Street to Cumberland Gardens, and met up with the road through to old Stonehouse (Ha'penny bridge) and through to Union Street and straight along to the new Plymouth City Centre. This left only a few tiny shops in Marlborough Street to act as a sop to the people of Devonport, plus what remained in Albert Road after the dockyard had taken the south side of the bottom half, and many of these have all but closed now. So the dear old Devonport that I knew as a boy has gone, and with it the better part of the community spirit of the old town. With the demise of that, the various other institutions which made it up became redundant. At one time before the Blitz, there were five cinemas in Devonport: the Criterion, Hippodrome, Electric, Forum, Tivoli, and the Alhambra Theatre. The fact that Devonport could at one time support all these, to say nothing of a branch of Woolworths, British Home Stores, and Marks & Spencer, goes to show what a thriving little town it was.

The decline has been and is progressive, and very little is left of old Devonport. Even the old Prince of Wales Hospital which served the area so well for so many years ceased to exist as such, but enough of it was left and adapted to provide more desirable up-to-date housing, to show that with a little ingenuity the old hospital could have served the community for many years to come if the same amount of money and imagination had been lavished on it, instead of building the multi-million-pound impersonal, tasteless monolith which Plymouth has been saddled with for future generations. A building singularly lacking in taste and imagination, and certainly no more efficient. It is also lacking a feeling of closeness and community that the old hospitals had.

Devonport was also sufficiently important to warrant a branch office of the local paper, the *Evening Herald*, furniture shops, Lazarus, and Garretts, also photographers, who did very good business from naval families. I know that my mother had our pictures taken fairly regularly to send to my father so that he would be able to see how his little family was faring and growing. One of my vivid memories was "Handbag day". This was mother's fortnightly visit to the Post Office in Albert Road to collect her naval allowance. This was an allowance made to naval wives from their husband's pay. At one time, there was a minimum amount that a man was required to allow his wife but there was also a maximum set, which ensured that the man had sufficient to pay for the necessities of clothing and to keep himself looking well turned out. Mother would then return home, and out would come the little tins, each with its label, RENT, COAL, GAS, DOCTOR, INSURANCE, CLOTHES, and several other things including even one for the cost of recharging the accumulator or battery for the old radio set, which was our only source of entertainment. I hated missing *Children's Hour*. All the money was placed on the old green baize table cloth, and when allocated to the respective tins was always finally checked and put away. The remaining few coins were carefully put away with the remark "and that's ours", which meant that we could have some little treat.

The little treat was sometimes an ice cream from the Exmouth Café, just on the corner in Portland Road, served by Jenny, whom I thought I was in love with, but on hindsight I am now more inclined to think that it was more likely that it was her ice cream that attracted me, particularly the day that she gave me a very large portion, and I went home to mother and told her "Jenny gave me a penny ice cream for a ha'penny!" Sometimes the treat was to meet Aunt Flo in Plymouth, and go into a tea shop for a cuppa and a piece of cake. Aunt Flo was the widow of one of my father's older brothers, George. Uncle George had died in Mesopotamia in 1916 of enteric fever, while on war service, leaving Aunt Flo a childless widow with a pittance of a pension. But more of that presently.

These little interludes would not mean much today, and it would be almost impossible to relate them to these times. Perhaps it was because people's expectations were less; they had to be, because real treats cost far more than they could afford, but the pleasure derived was out of all proportion to the cost and effort, and the fact that so many people remember those times with pleasure must signify that they were simple, and stemmed from a strength of character more wholesome than exists now.

From Milne Villas, we made what was to be our last move while Dad was still in the Navy. That was across the park to Marlborough House, which was beside the gate of Granby army barracks and opposite the Prince of Wales Hospital. Once again, we were very happy there and I was still able to spend many hours in my beloved Devonport Park. One of the things that I remember most was looking from the park out over the Hamoaze, watching the warships entering and leaving. When the home fleet returned to harbour I was taken down to Mutton Cove to watch them come in from the Sound and straighten up for the approach to the Hamoaze and dockyard. My father served in HMS *Renown* during the Royal Tour, and I remember that she couldn't enter harbour at any time she pleased. She displaced 32,000 tons and could only enter on a high tide, and I believe she touched bottom ever so slightly on more than one occasion, but I remember what a lovely sight she made, and the sound of her Royal Marine band playing her signature tune, "Happy days are here again", and believe me, they were. I believe the happiest time of my younger life was then. I had my mother and young brother, and my father, and I was proud of the fact that he was a navy man. My mother often spoke of the time when she would walk to the RN Barracks to meet my dad coming ashore. In those times, all the men came ashore in uniform. They formed line abreast and marched up the slope towards the barrack gates, saluting the officer of the watch as they passed, and broke off a little way from the gate.

On one particular day, it appears, I went with my mother as I often did, to meet him. An acquaintance stopped and spoke to her. After a few minutes, she said to me "And where are you off to young man?". I replied, "I'm going to meet my daddy." - "Oh!" she replied, "going to meet Daddy from work?" I was most indignant. "No," I replied emphatically, "my daddy doesn't work, my daddy's in the Navy!" There was a lot of infantile logic somewhere in my reply.

I could never remember the time when I didn't want to join the Navy. To me, none of the other services could compare. My father always loved the service, and believed in the British Empire, King and Country and inculcated that into me, although I believe, not deliberately. Since the time that I have been able to think for myself I have tried to analyse my feelings on the matter, and be completely honest about it, because I think that it is wrong to take on attitudes and opinions simply because they are propounded by people you love or like or respect, and God knows, I had all those feelings for my father. But after deep reflection, I have to say that I share his views in this matter. I firmly believe that the British Empire was one of the greatest forces for good that this world has ever known. Yes, instances of excess can be pointed at with perfect justification; some of them indefensible. But in the broadest sense, we left every part of the Empire better than we found it. Where there was no justice we left a judicial system which, although not perfect was a whole lot better than that which we found. The same can be applied to medicine, commerce and engineering, both civil and mechanical, and education. None of this would have been possible, indeed, even started without the Royal Navy. In those days, to me, the Royal Navy was Devonport and its dockyard, and Devonport and its dockyard was the Royal Navy, and always will be.

Chapter Sixteen

The Old Ships

One cannot talk of the old navy without mentioning the old ships. I say the old ships as distinct from "Old ships". The first is an old ship in the sense that it is not new, or that she is one of the ships that you have served on in the past. In the other sense, an "Old ship" is a shipmate who served with you on a previous ship, e.g. "Knocker White an' me are old ships". Old ships in all senses inspire affection and loyalty, usually to a quite high degree. It is very unusual to hear a sailor run down his old ship, or for that matter an old shipmate, unless of course she was not a "happy ship". To anyone who has not served in the Navy, it may not seem all that important, but anyone who has would quickly put you right on that score. There is nothing more miserable than an unhappy ship. It is a state of mind that infects every living soul aboard, and there is no possible way that one can avoid it. Unlike being ashore, where you can get out of each other's way, you are stuck there, and there is no relief, and, once the rot has set in there is no cure. But thankfully, an unhappy ship is the exception rather than the rule; it has to be if life on board is to be bearable.

All ships have a character of their own as do people. I have met people who think that this is just another sailor's yarn.

It isn't. It is not only possible, but more likely than not, that sister ships, built to the same plan, with exactly the same dimensions, behave in an entirely different manner at sea. One will roll her guts out in anything like a seaway, while another will stick her nose into a head sea, and come up shaking herself like a dog; another will answer the helm almost immediately, while her sister will make up her mind a fortnight later. A real old salt once said, "That's why they call a ship *she*. Like all women, they are often unpredictable, and no two of them are alike. You have to give them all your attention all the time, if you don't they'll catch you unawares and make you wish you had. They can make your life a misery if you let them, and there are times that you wish that you had never clapped eyes on them, but for some reason you can't keep away from them, and one thing is certain: you can never forget them."

I have known many ships over the years, but only served in one before being invalided out of the service. I have nevertheless taken a great personal interest in everything naval since. My father served in ten different ships during his more than twenty-two years service. First, the old *Benbow* for over three years, followed over the years by *Australia*, *Emperor of India* and *Ajax*, all of which were old coal burners; then *Ramillies*, *Herald*, *Hermes*, *Renown*, *Witch*, a destroyer, and finally, after being called back from pension, *Courageous*, in which he lost his life. To me, each of these ships were special and of great interest.

Hiraeth

Would that I could see you, and relive times of old.
Days I thought so ordinary, and knew not they were gold.
To see your face and see your smile,
and laugh and talk with you awhile.

But I can never do so, or experience the joy,
that once I had so long ago, when I was still a boy.
'Twas when my need was greatest that you could not be there,
to counsel and advise me, to love me and to care.

O'er half a century later I still can feel the pain,
and I would give 'most anything to see you once again.
But when my life is over, I pray that I can be,
somewhere beyond this vale of tears, again to be with thee.

P.E. Gibbings

Chapter Seventeen

The First Lonely Winter

That winter was long, and in a sort of way, lonely. I remember a continual gnawing at my insides that seemed almost physical, and a feeling which I can only describe as a vacuum in my chest. My father had spent so many years away in the service, that until he pensioned he was just a regular letter in the door, or an exciting short interlude before again going away. But for the last few years, to have him there to talk to and to ask things was wonderful, and I just couldn't grasp that I would never see him again. There was also my constant fear of losing Mum. When we had lived in Stoke, we often saw the crocodile of children going in and out of the dockyard orphanage at the top of Albert Road, and on occasions when I'd perhaps not behaved as I should, she would remind me how fortunate my brother and I were to have parents. I sometimes wonder whether she realised how much that upset me, and instilled a fear within me that I could perhaps one day be in that unfortunate position; in the winter of 1939, it was a fear that constantly haunted me.

My melancholia, for that was what it was, persisted for a long time and I couldn't seem to conquer it. It was not that I was always miserable; there were times that I would snap out of it, but only to return to that dreadful pit of despair. There is no word in the English language that adequately sums up this state of mind, or rather feeling, but there is a lovely little word in the Welsh language that covers it very adequately. It has no direct translation, but describes a feeling of nostalgia, longing, homesickness or grief, it is *hiraeth*. There is no better word to describe my own feelings; a dreadful longing that filled my every day, tinged with the naïve hope of a young boy that even now it may not be true, but knowing deep down that it was.

It was a feeling that never left me. Now, all these years later, it has been given a posh sounding scientific name; post-traumatic stress syndrome, and one can have counselling and therapy, but I think it is about fifty years too late for us. I say *us* because I have a friend who feels exactly as I do, the only difference is that he never knew his father; he was born after his father died in *Courageous*. In a letter to me he said , "I never knew him, but I missed him. He wasn't there when I needed him, when I was growing up, but he was my father and I loved him." Both he and I are grown men, and he is over ten years younger than me, and we have both served in the Navy, but we still have that feeling of *hiraeth*, and there must be many others who feel as we do.

It is true that every experience has value, both good and bad, and from it one learns lessons which help to form character; the only problem is that our morale sometimes suffers while we are learning them. This was true in my case, the shock was greater because not only had I lost my father, but we had to move back to Plymouth, and that entailed changing schools of course, and I had never been so happy as I was at Stag Lane School in Middlesex.

While Plymouth was my birthplace and the only city that I loved, in those days its schools, at least those that I attended, left a lot to be desired. Compared to Stag Lane, the school that I attended on our return to Plymouth came way down the list with regard to the quality of teaching, or rather, it would be more fair to say that the particular teacher of my class came way down the list. I'd had a great deal of sickness over the previous year, and was in a very poor physical state. Consequently, I was a long way behind my peers with regard to education, and particularly regarding mathematics, which seemed to be the yardstick by which all our education seemed to be assessed. I was brilliant at history, a subject that always held my interest, and a very good speller and reader. Geography too was a great favourite of mine, but maths... oh dear! The teacher - incidentally the only *male* teacher in the school - was very dour and sarcastic. He had his favourites - two particular girls, whom he delighted in holding up as paragons of mathematical virtue. One of these young ladies was extremely nice and never attempted to capitalise on her ability. The other was quite the opposite. It would only be fair to mention that I was not alone in my misery. Another lad shared the scholastic doghouse with me, and we suffered greatly at the hands of Mr P.

At that time, about three months after my father's death, I was just about at my lowest ebb with regard to my loss. I missed him to the extent that it almost hurt physically. It was as though I had reached the nadir of my misery. We had that morning taken a periodic test in mental arithmetic, and I had achieve the distinction of attaining my lowest score; three correct answers from twenty questions. We each corrected our own papers. When he had ascertained those with high scores, the teacher then asked those with less than ten correct to raise their hands. He then made each one read their score out loud. When I had admitted to only three, he slowly walked to the back of the class where I was seated and, taking me by the ear, dragged me out to the front of the class and literally shook me by the ear. I had never seen him so angry. His face seemed to be twisted into a sneer, and I shall never forget his words: "Look at it, look at it, it'll never be fit for anything but sweeping the roads." He then caned me. I do not believe that he could ever have understood how utterly destroyed I felt. It was something I never forgot. But fate is sometimes kind. Over twenty years later, when I was well established in my profession and certainly far from being the poor miserable little soul that he tormented, I had the good fortune to almost literally bump into him in the street. He remembered me but couldn't quite put a name to me. I reminded him of his words and took great pleasure in doing so. He replied that it didn't look as though it had done me any harm. I answered to the effect that had his prophecy been fulfilled, he would have been the first thing to have been put in the dustbin. Revenge is sweet. I have always contrasted this man to the wonderful teachers that I had at Stag Lane School. They were real professionals.

It may be that I was too harsh in my judgement. I later learned that he was an embittered man, having been passed over for the headship of the school, and perhaps, as in my case and others, it had left scars, which to say the least can colour our views of others. I have to admit that the harshness of my life at that time tended to make me a little less sympathetic to others than I would otherwise have been.

The year turned, and it was early spring in 1940. The country had accepted that we really were at war. Another of our big ships had been lost when *Royal Oak* was torpedoed by Günther Prien inside Scapa Flow: a massive blow to our morale. Although it was a terrible tragedy for the families, it had the effect of removing any complacency regarding the impregnability of what was regarded as a very secure anchorage for capital ships, and enlarged our small club of those who had lost someone in the war, a club which was not so exclusive now. For our family, we had only two rooms for the three of us, and the use of a bathroom. It can be imagined how much my mother felt this after having her own house. Also the loss of income was a tremendous blow. My father was a Post Office civil servant, and, of course had his naval pension:- an income of over six pounds per week. To be reduced to less than two pounds per week was a very large drop; God knows how my mother managed. But she did, and never complained to us.

With the spring of 1940 came our first little piece of luck. Plymouth City Council, God bless them, offered us a two-bedroom flat in St Budeaux. This was a striking contrast to the lovely house we had in Queensbury, but at least we were all together again and could make a start in trying to mend our lives.

The sudden drastic fall in income was so great that my mother had no choice but to work, and with the country on a war footing it was of course not too difficult to find. There was the Naval Dockyard taking in female workers and also the Royal Naval Armament Depot at Bull Poirt and Ernesettle. The latter, being within walking distance of our little flat at St Budeaux, was the obvious choice. Even a saving on the bus fare at that time meant a difference to her meagre income.

I think that this was the most dreary time, my mother at work in the inspection department of the RNAD and my brother and I at local schools. This was even more difficult for her because my school was on split time: mornings one week and afternoons the next, while my brother was on normal time, and mother on different shifts at the RNAD. Unlike other families we had no relatives in Plymouth anywhere near, so that there was no choice but to struggle on.

Chapter Eighteen

The War – the Early Days

During this time, mother had registered for war work. Everyone over the age of eighteen had to register. All males who were medically fit were taken into the armed services, as were a large number of young women, and the remainder were put into the many other forms of war work. Mother worked in the Royal Naval Armament factory at Bull Point, and later at nearby Ernesettle as an inspector of naval ordnance, where she remained until well after the war, having attained the position of chief inspector. This was no mean achievement in view of the fact that her only employment prior to her marriage to my father was as a nurse. But she could not afford to go back to nursing because she could not afford to live on a nurse's pay.

So began years of dreary toil, with very little to look forward to. Long hours on often dangerous work, with periods of night work took their toll, but I do not remember her ever having any time off apart from her meagre annual leave, which during the war was very limited.

It was in the spring of 1940 that I went away to the Royal Hospital School at Holbrook in Suffolk, and my brother was evacuated to Totnes with family friends from my mother's younger days.

So in the space of a few months our circumstances had changed from being a very happy suburban family, with an income which at that time was considered to be very much more than adequate, to a bereaved and traumatised one, which, apart from brief visits when I was on leave and could travel up to Totnes to see my brother, was not to be properly reunited until the end of the war.

Another factor which completely changed our life was that the insurance company with whom my father's life was insured refused to pay out the normal settlement on the grounds that the additional war risk premium had not been paid, and instead, only returned the premiums already paid; a fraction of the amount that would have been payable if death had been of natural causes. The refusal of this company to honour what was a moral, even if not a legal, obligation altered the whole course of our lives. This company still exists, and of course the people responsible are long gone, but I could never bring myself to have any dealings with them. I have always held that the morality of any situation should always take precedence to legality; legality is a system devised by man, and while it is a genuine attempt to regulate the affairs of man, and man has not been able to find a better one yet, morality, is something ingrained in our souls by God, and is therefore absolute. No man can ever improve on that.

The first winter of the war drew on, and it was only a month later when the old battleship *Royal Oak* was sunk in a daring attack by Günther Prien in U47 when he entered Scapa Flow, followed by the armed merchant cruiser *Rawalpindi* only six weeks after that. This, with the bad news from France and preparation for what was obviously going to be a very long siege, did nothing for the morale of the country, and even less for those of us who had already suffered, and my memories of the period up to the time of Dunkirk are a little hazy. Probably this was in part due to the fact that I was settling into my new life at school, and we were almost cut off from the outside world, having no newspapers or radio, and never ever going outside the confines of the school grounds on pain – quite literally – of three strokes of the cane if we were caught doing so.

Then came the Battle of Britain. We often saw the German bombers as they made their way to London, and saw the vapour trails of dogfights as they were chased and harried by our fighters. The school is situated at Holbrook in Suffolk on the banks of the River Stour. It occupies some three hundred acres and has a very high tower which can be seen for many miles around. It is known that the bombers took their bearing for London from the tower, therefore we had a grandstand view of them approaching although they always went over at a very high altitude.

The period between the end of 1939 and the Blitz, with the exception of Dunkirk, passed with a steady war of attrition, and constant minor bad and demoralising news. However, we got used to it and our strength gradually grew, till we found that we were becoming part of an increasingly large family of those who had lost loved ones, and so were no longer treated with the sympathy that we encountered at the beginning.

I still feel that my mother must have suffered far more than I could have ever understood. I was away in a life of discipline that left little time for feeling lonely, but she came home after every shift to a cold and empty flat, with blackout curtains still drawn as she had left them when she had gone to work in the dark. How she must have contrasted this with her lovely suburban home so recently acquired after years of rented rooms, and my father roaming the world, and having attained their dream, only to have it torn away from her so cruelly after such a short time. I have always felt that I would not have been able to have borne such a blow. But she did, and although I frequently saw her near the depths of despair, she never gave in, and never complained. While I was at school, there was a steady flow of parcels with little luxuries of cake and food. With all the wartime shortages, God knows how she managed it. I am sure now that she must, many times, have gone short herself. I know that at the time I was very grateful, but alas, like many others, didn't always say so.

Chapter Nineteen

The War Ends

Towards the end, when the tables had been well and truly turned, things happened thick and fast. Not a day passed without fresh victories and more evidence of the total collapse of Nazi Germany. But even then, fighting was as fierce as it had ever been, and still men were being killed and maimed. But we knew that the end was not far off, and after the awful ordeal that we had been through we began to think about what would come after. One thing was certain: we were going to celebrate! After all those years of death, destruction, sorrow and shortages we were going to have a short breather, a knees-up, a good bash. Yes, we knew that we had work to do, and years of rebuilding, both of our war-torn country and our lives, but after what we had gone through we were going to have a good old shin-dig, and nobody was going to stop us.

I was seventeen when the war ended, and like many others I had had a rough time, with none of the things that youngsters of our age had been used to before the war, and we were going to celebrate. I well remember the night of VE Day. We had learned from Rediffusion, our local radio, that there was dancing on the Hoe that evening, and I was determined to go, and I asked Mum whether she would come too. I can recall her words now: "No, you go on and enjoy yourself, I've got nothing to celebrate." I'm ashamed to say that I *did* go on, but I didn't enjoy myself. I kept telling myself that I couldn't do anything if I had stayed at home, but it didn't help, and I've felt ashamed of it ever since, and it damned well serves me right, and the fact that she never reproached me makes it *worse*, not better.

I am sure that as time went on, and the men started coming home as demobilisation increased, she felt the full impact of her condition. Indeed, it seemed that war widows could really, as far as the government was concerned, fend for themselves; they had their meagre pensions, and the rest of the country was busy with other things, and they were really only a part of the detritus of war – a part that could not be cleared away, much as they would have liked to.

So, Mother fended for herself. She was still for a short while employed at the armament depot, and when women were dispensed with there, she was one of the last to leave. At least the Admiralty were considerate enough to dispense with the married women first. She went from there to a local branch of the Chain libraries, and despite the very low wage remained at their Devonport branch as manageress until they closed down. There followed several years as receptionist at a motor school, where she remained until she retired at the age of sixty. She then had her old age pension to add to her war widow's pension, but although her war pension was not taxable on its own, if she earned any further money, the two would be added, and the war widow's pension was taxed as, would you believe, unearned income. Although this was not generally known, it is nevertheless a fact, and, I believe, one of the greatest insults to the dead of the two world wars that could be imagined.

Blame for the contempt shown to war widows lies equally at the door of every government since the end of the war. They could all have done something about it, but failed to. Indeed, I rather think that it would be more accurate to say that they had no intention of doing so. There is no real political kudos to be gained in courting the war widows lobby.

It would have been a good idea if, after the war, or indeed during the war, the government could have had a small distinctive medal or badge struck for war widows. I have seen many a veteran wearing a little silver lapel badge, with the inscription, 'FOR LOYAL SERVICE' and GR inscribed on it. Why could there not have been one for the war widows. After all, the veterans did come home, and had something to come back to. Yes, they had it rough, but they did have *hope* to sustain them: the war widow had nothing to lock forward to. Also, such a badge would have been a reminder to the various tradesmen and shopkeepers of the need for that little extra when there occasionally was some. Of all who survived the war, I do not think that any paid a higher price than the war widow; a price that most continue to pay for the rest of their lives.

The sacrifice of these courageous women is one that I have always been very aware of, and there have been two occasions when I have had the opportunity to do something about it, albeit in a small way. The first was just after the war, when I was on leave from the Navy. I was in uniform because I had no civilian clothes at that time, having grown cut of all the civilian clothes that I had. My mother and I were in Plymouth when we saw a queue outside a greengrocer's shop. At that time when one saw a queue, one joined it first and found out what it was for after. In this case there was a notice declaring that there were oranges for sale, one on each ration book. When the queue reached the counter, the man serving asked how many books. "Two," my mother replied. At which he proceeded to put a quantity of cabbage leaves into her bag and then two oranges, and charged for both the leaves and the oranges. Now this was illegal, and a trick often tried to get rid of the rubbish and charge for it. More often than not they got away with it because people were desperate to have things like oranges because they had not seen any since the war began, and this was so in Mother's case. The other reason was that the majority of people didn't like making a scene. This was also the case with my mother, but certainly not with me. I reminded the man that this was an offence, and that we did not want the cabbage leaves. I was told that if we didn't want the leaves we wouldn't get the oranges. To say that I was angry was an understatement. I thought of all the privations that my mother had suffered in the war and in no uncertain language told him. He in turn told us that we were holding up the queue and that we could take it or leave it. I replied that if we didn't get oranges then nobody would because I would personally stamp on the lot and him too. My poor mother was upset and begged me not to do anything silly. Finally, I managed to persuade her to go and get a policeman, which in those days, particularly in the middle of Plymouth, one could. She did, leaving me in the shop arguing with the shopkeeper and telling him in no uncertain terms that my father had given his life so that rubbish like him could grow fat out of selling trash to war widows, and breaking the law at the same time. It was only a very short while before the bobby arrived, a policeman of the old stamp. He listened to both sides and proceeded to give me a dressing down for threatening to give the shopkeeper an orange suppository. He then turned to the shopkeeper and told him that I was right and he was committing an offence and could be heavily fined. We walked out of the shop with two lovely oranges, the first that we had seen since the outbreak of war – but that wasn't the reason they tasted so good!

The second occasion was when I learned from Aunt Flo, the widow of one of my father's older brothers, that ever since his death in Mesopotamia in 1916 while on war service she had received a war widow's pension for my uncle at the rank of corporal. She had been in contact with the War Office over the years with regard to this and had been told that he was a corporal and that was that. She showed me one of his letters in which he stated that he had been promoted to the rank of acting company sergeant major for the voyage to Mesopotamia, and he had even quoted the date and number of the regimental order. She was also in possession of a photograph of him in the full uniform of company sergeant major complete with the red sash. Now it is a strict regulation that a man cannot be promoted to any acting rank until he has been fully confirmed in the previous rank. Hence, Uncle George must have been fully confirmed as a sergeant to have been made an acting company sergeant major. I was at that time the chairman of a branch of the British Legion (it had not at that time been honoured with the title of Royal British Legion). I took the matter up with the help of our pensions officer and Commander Douglas Marshall, our local MP. The War Office argued that the records of the Second Devon Regiment had been destroyed after thirty years and that there was no evidence. The case was won on the grounds that we had evidence in writing and a photograph, and unless they could provide evidence that the man concerned had been deprived of his rank by a court martial or other disciplinary body, then game, set and match. My aunt received an increase in her pension of two shillings per week, the difference between the pension of a corporal and a sergeant, backdated to the time of his death in 1916.

In these two stories it can be seen that war widows have for years been the victims of injustice by both the authorities and in everyday life. In my conversation with Kapt. Schuhart I learned that German war widows enjoyed pensions that would be the envy of our people, to say nothing of other privileges in transport concessions. A *Face the Facts* programme, investigating the plight of war widows, stated that Japanese war widows received three times the rate of pension granted by the British government. But the worst story of the lot was of a titled lady, who lived in a castle, and whose husband was awarded the Victoria Cross posthumously for an act of extreme gallantry. She actually suffered ruination by death duties, and into the bargain when she received her pension book was asked not to draw it unless she had to. She was appalled by the request, as one would imagine she would have been. She stated that apart from the insult, she had to draw the pension - she had no other choice. One wonders whether or not she was surcharged because the envelope had no stamp on it. The programme suggested that the whole set-up of widows' pensions seemed to be structured to positively force them into a second marriage, particularly when they were given a year's pension as a dowry upon their remarriage.

The employment market at that time was also heavily weighted against them. Who wanted a middle-aged woman, sometimes with a couple of kids? Employers in those times would not offer work to a woman who might ask for time off to take children to the doctor or the dentist, or nurse them when they were sick. There were no employment protection laws at that time.

There was surely no group in society more disadvantaged than those who had paid the highest price of anyone in that war. In the case of *Courageous*, there was a very high number of widows whose husbands had already served their full time for pension, and indeed, like my father, had already served right through the First World War; he served in the battleship *Benbow* from October 1914 until December 1917, and fought in Admiral Jellicoe's squadron at Jutland, and in the battle cruiser *Australia* until after hostilities ceased. He and many others had earned their pensions fully, and the nation already owed them a debt. They should never have been sent to sea. In terms of sea warfare they were old men, and in a life-threatening situation such as the sinking of their ship, their chances of survival were not rated as being very high.

Only a comparatively small number of war widows remarried. During the war, most of the men of their age were serving, and they themselves were bringing up children. Also, those men who were perhaps available had no wish to take on a ready-made family. After the war most of them were still out at work from necessity rather than choice, and time had passed them by even further. Indeed, in almost every aspect of post-war life - work, income and marriage prospects - even if they *had* been so inclined, they were in a 'no win' situation.

Chapter Twenty

The Old Navy

My whole life has been lived in and around the Navy. In my early days I was in close contact all the time. I seldom saw my father out of uniform, apart from the few times on leave. At that time men left and arrived home in uniform. Most of our friends and acquaintances were naval families, indeed the Navy was one big family, although it was really in two parts.

The first part was the service itself, the officers and men.

It had a code, albeit unwritten, to which every man subscribed. Loyalty to the service, each other and the ship. All problems, feuds, fights, moans, groans and complaints were kept in the family, and invariably sorted out and settled in the Navy's own inimitable way. If you transgressed against the service you were dealt with. Usually very quickly and nearly always fairly, although many didn't think so at the time. But the service didn't bear grudges; a man could nearly always redeem himself unless he repeated the offence, or the first offence was of a very serious nature. You were frequently told that the Navy had a routine for everything, and always looked after its own, and it did.

I witnessed such an instance during my own part one training.

This consisted of basic naval training, i.e. square-bashing, basic seamanship, communications, damage control, and general naval routine and law. Although I had spent four years in a naval school I still had to go through basic training. During this we were all chivvied around and bawled at in the old time-honoured fashion. I was used to it to the extent that it no longer made me unduly upset or reduced me to a nervous wreck, but I knew better than to ignore it. Indeed, most of the class after a few weeks were beginning to accept that this was all part of the old routine. "If you can't take a joke, you shouldn't have joined!" However, one particular morning one of the class, Chambers, a pretty ordinary sort of bloke, who normally never had any problems, seemed to be attracting some undue attention from the instructor. He didn't seem to be paying much attention to drill commands, and was half a second late in moving, getting out of step and being generally slack. After a few sharp words which didn't seem to produce an improvement, the instructor really bawled at him eyeball to eyeball, telling him that if he didn't pull himself together, he'd spend an hour or two doubling around the parade ground. At this Chambers fell apart, and tears started to fall. The whole thing was so dramatic that it was obvious that something was very wrong. Chambers still stood at attention, trying hard to control himself, but his features trembling. The old chief's voice softened, and he asked, "What's up, son?" Chambers couldn't seem to answer. After a few seconds, another lad quietly said, "He had a letter from home this morning, Chief, about his mum." At this, the chief very quietly said "OK, son, just walk on over to the divisional office and wait for me." In less than an hour, Chambers was on his way home on compassionate leave. A quick check was made by the padre and it was verified that his mother had been taken seriously ill and sent to hospital. The Navy really *did* look after its own, and behaved in the same way as most families. Dad can clip your ear, but nobody else can.

At that time there were many men in the service who had no other home. They were mostly orphans who had perhaps been brought up in institutions; perhaps a series of such places. Indeed, I knew several who had been sent to Brixham Orphanage at the age of seven, and had then gone on into the Royal Hospital School at Greenwich, and Holbrook, and from there straight into the Navy. In many cases, these boys had never had a home in the normally accepted sense. The service was the only home they knew. When came the normal leave periods, these lads had nowhere to go; as one old salt said of one such lad, "Poor little bugger, he didn't have any come from or go to." There were quite a number of these lads in the twenties and thirties – products of orphanages and homes, who quite literally had no family or relatives of any kind.

At the Royal Hospital School, boys in this position were billeted with families within a few miles radius of the school for the period of leave. The majority of these families were wonderful people who looked after boys well – indeed, to a far greater extent than required of them by the terms of the arrangement. But after leaving the school and entering the Navy, the arrangement ended because the lad could be drafted anywhere. So the service granted what was known as lower deck leave. This meant that when leave periods came, he could, if he wished, remain aboard the ship to sleep and have meals, but proceed ashore as and when he pleased without any restrictions, apart from the fact that he had to be clear of the mess deck for rounds,

The hands would be rousted out by 0630 and turned to, but the man on leave would be allowed to have his breakfast aboard, after which he could please himself what he did. He could return to the mess deck after rounds or inspection if he wished, but could go ashore provided he handed in his station card in the usual way. Each man had what was known as a station card which showed his name, rank and watch (port or starboard), and his part of ship. Without your station card you were not allowed ashore, and you collected it immediately you returned aboard. If you were picked up for an offence while aboard, your card would be taken from you. It would only be returned after your offence had been dealt with. In this way, a man under punishment or threat of punishment would not be able to leave the ship or establishment until he had been dealt with, or if the chief or petty officer who had taken it decided whether or not to proceed any further with the offence. In this way, a man could be warned and allowed ashore later than normal,

Another reason for the station card system was that it was always known in any emergency who was aboard or ashore. This was a good system and worked well. As Chiefy always said, "The Navy has a routine for everything." If ever any new situation cropped up and there was no system already, you could bet your sweet life that there would be a new routine to cope with it in a brace of shakes, and it worked! Any man who thought that he could buck the system would soon learn that many a better man had tried, and the result was nearly always failure. In the very few cases where they did succeed in pulling a fast one, the hole was blocked with a speed that made your head spin. There is an apocryphal story told that demonstrates the point. On Sundays, in the Navy, divisions are held. All the ship's company fall in by divisions and are inspected by their divisional officers to see that they are clean and properly dressed, and that the mess decks are clear to be inspected. Then there follows a religious service according to denominations. The chiefs give the order

"Roman Catholics fall out to the left, Methodists to the right, Presbyterians, and Church of Scotland to the rear." That leaves the Church of England in one group, and the others are marched away to their various places of worship. In the story, two bright sparks thought that if they changed their religion to Muslim, they would not have to attend any church or religious service because there was no provision made for them. However, one had to formally request to change religion. This they did, and their request was of course granted; the Navy has always recognised freedom of religious choice. The following Sunday the two lads thought that after divisions, when all the other men were marched off to their various places of worship, they would be able to nip back down to their mess deck for a crafty smoke and a read before Sunday lunch. But after inspection the divisional officer gave the usual order, "Carry on, Chief." Chiefy came out with the usual spiel, "Roman Catholic's fall out to the left, Methodists fall out to the right, Presbyterians and Church of Scotland fall out to the rear, and Muslims muster on the fo'c'sle with their prayer mats!"

The sailor has always been adept at spinning a yarn. The real trick for the listener is to decide which to believe, and which to take with a modicum of Sodium Chloride. The strange thing is that very often the ones that seem to come under the heading of fairy tales are true, and vice versa!

The Navy is quite different to the other services in many ways, and for a multitude of reasons - some obvious, and some not so obvious. This is not to say that the traditions, practices or ways of doing things in the other services are wrong or in any way inferior. They are just different. For a start, at sea, the men live in far closer proximity to each other. There is no way that one can avoid one's shipmates, much less one's messmates. You see the same people day after day; some you may like and some you may not, but it makes no difference, you have to try and get on with each other. You make the best of it. It says a great deal for the majority of men who form the ship's company of most ships that there is very seldom any really open friction. If there is, then the messmates of the men involved very soon put a stop to it before it comes to a head, and those concerned are soon made aware that it won't be tolerated.

The Navy between the wars was a world apart. At sea your space consisted of the mahogany locker which ran round the bulkheads (walls) of the mess, and formed a continuous seat. Each man was allocated a locker, and the lid or seat lifted to allow storage space for his kit. Your hammock was lashed and stowed in the morning, and only taken out and slung when you turned in. During the evenings you would sit on your locker, and the mess tables were rigged for you to write or play cards on.

There were slight variations according to the type or class of ship and the number of men in the complement. All the big ships and even some of the smaller ones had men who ran small businesses aboard, quite legally. For instance, there was nearly always a barber who would cut your hair for a few pence, and the chippy (carpenter) who would make a hammock stretcher for you. This kept the sides of your hammock from closing over when you climbed in. There were short courses that men could take in boot and shoe repairing (Ship's snob), and on the bigger ships, a *dhobi* firm, a word taken from the Hindi word for washing; two or more men would undertake to wash, dry and iron clothing for the ship's company for a fee. There were many other ways that men supplemented their meagre pay. Many were the initiatives that sprang up, and more than one man made enough money during a long commission to invest in a house when he got home. There were even bookies' firms set up, but they were of course illegal and the punishments were severe for those caught.

The most important thing was to keep busy, that way there was less mischief born of boredom. Sailors are the most resourceful people in the world, and often the most clever with their hands. Model making was one of the most common pastimes, and I have seen some of the intricate and lovely models made aboard ship, to say nothing of knitting and embroidery. One of the most incongruous things that I have ever witnessed took place one day on a train. I was only fifteen, and returning to the naval school from leave on the train from Plymouth to Paddington. The train was packed with servicemen. The compartment was full and there were men standing in the corridors. I was sat between a petty officer and a massive three-badge stoker. He was big, and I mean *big*. We were sat opposite two elderly ladies, who were each flanked by sailors. As the train started we all settled down and the compartment was soon filled with smoke. My large companion produced a very large pipe and proceeded to fill it with thick ship's twist – navy tobacco, often, as in this case soaked in illicitly saved rum ration, and dried. As an ex-pipe smoker I can vouch that it is one of the most delightful smokes that one could ever wish for, even though it is, to say the least, very pungent and overpowering for the non-smoker, particularly in a confined space. A match was applied, and the pipe was drawing well, a fact that was shown by the expression of sheer pleasure on the face of my large friend. He then reached above his head and pulled a small ditty bag from the luggage rack, thrust his huge ham-like fist in, and withdrew some knitting! It was not ordinary knitting, but the most intricate piece of Fair Isle knitting that I have ever seen, with a pattern. Following the pattern, he proceeded to knit, slowly, but deliberately, and without hesitation, occasionally glancing at his pattern. I watched for a while, until I caught sight of one of the old ladies. Her face was a picture. She was fascinated, and clearly filled with admiration. She continued to watch him for some time, until, feeling her eyes on him, he stopped. He looked at her and after a few seconds, seeming to wonder why she was looking at him so intently, said, "Oh, sorry, missus, is my pipe bovverin' you?" The old lady looked a little embarrassed. "Oh, no, no," she replied. "I was intrigued with your knitting. I have never seen such an intricate pattern as that. It looks most difficult; I do a lot of knitting, but I don't think I could manage a pattern that difficult." There followed a quiet conversation between the two of them in which our large companion showed her some of the various techniques involved in the particular piece of work. He then took a case off the rack and proceeded to show her the jumpers and other garments he had made during his last spell at sea. It transpired that he had six boys, and he spent all his spare time knitting all the woollen garments that they needed, and these set them up until he came home again. Heaven knows how he learned to knit, but from the remarks made by the old lady, he really was an expert.

Another form of amusement at sea was cockroach racing. I do not think that there was ever a ship without them. There was never any shortage of them in my ship. As the only medical rating, it was my job to disinfest both galleys, the sick bay, and the captain's quarters. This was done by spraying with DDT, but although this was done regularly, daily, every morning, by the evening they were back to full strength. However, the more agile of these were caught and raced. This was done by placing lanes or tracks on the deck, and releasing the competitors from a matchbox, as one would release a greyhound from a trap. One could encourage, cajole and threaten, but not touch a participant. The first to reach the other end won, but the penalty for the losers was - death!

To fully understand the attitudes of a sailor, one has to have personal experience of seafaring, or have been intimately involved with the service. Being a navy man is really a state of mind, reached first by a genuine desire to serve in the Royal Navy, and developed by a mix of training, attitudes, and experiences gained while serving with real navy men.

The real navy man is different from any other individual that you will ever meet. It is a state arrived at by living, working, eating, drinking and sleeping with the same group of men for long periods, in cramped conditions. You get to know each other very intimately; almost as well as you know your own family, and in some cases better. This was certainly the case when the average foreign commission was around two and a half years. Two and a half years away from your own family, with only letters for a link, and these had to be numbered so that you would know which one had been written first; often, number fifteen would arrive before fourteen. At times there would be no mail at all if the ship was detached from the remainder on some tedious task. The strain at times of these long periods away from home was intolerable. But very often, great friendships were forged in such conditions. Friendships that stood the test of time. The crew all relied on each other, and the men of a particular mess were really like a family, and, like all families, had their differences, which were settled within the family, and other messes (families) would never pry or interfere.

In a conversation a few years ago I heard someone ask an old seafarer whether he thought that seamen could be described as being at all religious. The old seaman thought for a moment, and replied, "I couldn't honestly answer that. Some may well be, but whether they are or not, I am sure that the majority are God-fearing." The average sailor is, with a few exceptions, not religious, but he has a very deep belief in the Almighty. "They that go down to the sea in ships..."

To describe life in the Navy between the two world wars and just after at all accurately would be almost an impossibility within the compass of one short work. It is something that one would actually have to experience. To begin with, the Navy has almost a language of its own, which bears very little relationship to civil life. It is a language which, like any other, has evolved over the years. Take names for instance. Nearly everyone is familiar with the nickname "Nobby" for anyone with the surname Clark, and "Wiggy" often goes with the name Bennett, but apart from special nicknames applied to people for some personal trait or idiosyncrasy, nicknames have never been so prevalent as they are in the Navy. The Army and the RAF have adopted some, but I think not on the same scale as the Navy. A few examples are Bagsy Baker, Pincher Martin, Knocker White, Bogey Knight, Tansy Lee, Pony Moore, Jumper Collins, Peggy O'Neill, Brigham Young, Darby Allen, Nick Carter, and Bungy Williams, to mention a few. There are many more, but some escape me; but few escape a nickname, and once given it sticks.

There are various words and terms which mean very little to the landsman or civilian. For instance, until a few years ago all ratings had an issue of duty-free tobacco. This could be either pipe or cigarette tobacco, and was issued in half-pound sealed tins, but prior to this it was collected in jam jars. Now, at one time, a firm called Tickler supplied the Navy with jam, and it was in their jars that the men collected their tobacco issue; hence, when a sailor offered a cigarette, he would say, "'ave a Tickler, mate." I think that any lady would have made a hasty exit at that stage! A tin of brass polish is still called a tin of Bluebell, after the name of the firm that supplied the Navy for a number of years. "The Andrew" is a term used by navy men meaning the Royal Navy, and is said to come from an eighteenth century officer by the name of Andrew Miller, who was so successful at impressing men into the Navy that he was said to own it. "Chock-a-block" means that Jack is fed up, and he often follows this up with "Roll on my twelve". The first period that a man signed on for was twelve years, after which he could sign on again for a further ten years to complete twenty-two years for pension, or leave the service, so "I'm chock-a-block, roll on my twelve" means "I'm fed up and I wish my twelve years was up". "Up spirits" was the order piped each day when the daily rum ration was issued. On small ships, orders over the Tannoy system are prefaced with a pipe from the bo'sun's call or whistle, so that the Quartermaster blows the call and orders "Up spirits". To which some wit will often reply, "Stand fast the Holy Ghost". The daily issue of rum in the Navy gave rise to a vocabulary of its own, and was often used as a currency on the lower deck. When a man did another a favour, he would be given "Sippers" if it was a small favour, or "Gulpers" if it was a bigger favour, or even the whole "Tot". This could often be for several days or a week, but to get a man's tot for a week he would probably want you to murder the first lieutenant! A sailor is never late, he is adrift. Tomorrow morning is tomorrow forenoon. When a man committed an offence, he was taken to the quarterdeck to be dealt with by either the first lieutenant or the captain, and once in front of that officer the order is given "Off cap". So if he is in danger of this happening, he is sometimes asked as a warning "Do you want to go aft with your bonnet off?" The term "Belay that" means stop whatever you are doing or disregard the last order, and to marry two ropes is to join them. The "Jaunty" is the master-at-arms, the "Buffer" is the chief bo'sun's mate, and "Jimmy the one" is the first lieutenant. A "Sea daddy" is an older or more experienced man that takes a younger or less experienced man under his wing and shows him the ropes (a term which in itself means that the man was shown which ropes to handle in a sailing vessel by an old hand). The list is endless, and each generation adds more. Having heard all these terms since childhood I have grown up with them, as any child grows up with a language, but I have always thought how confusing it must have been to anyone suddenly forced into the service as in wartime, without having had any contact with it previously. One thing is certain: the Royal Navy is a one-off. There is no other service that it can be fairly compared with, and certainly no other service inspires more loyalty among its members, or pride in having been a member.

Chapter Twenty-One

My Mother

If I had to use one word to describe my mother, it would have to be tranquil. It took a great deal to really upset her. Yes, she would become vexed, but I don't think I ever saw her lose her temper. The only job that she had after her marriage until my father's death was to look after her family, which she did so well in times that were anything but easy. She would always have little things to tell us about her younger days when she was an only child in Dawlish, and the people that she knew. She was a combination of common sense and compassion; intuition and intelligence; love and loyalty. Slow to anger, and quick to forgive. Her plump neat figure carried her clothing neatly and smartly; she was one of those rare people who could buy a cheap dress and attract compliments purely by the way she wore it. She could both walk with kings and talk with crowds and surrender nothing of her character. She had known sadness, losing her father when she was still a child, and her mother when a young adult, and her husband after only fourteen years of marriage at the opening shots of the Second World War. She grieved for her husband for the rest of her life, but not to the detriment of her two sons. I, the elder, was eleven, and my brother only seven when she started work in the Naval Armament Depot, but by the end of the war she had attained the position of chief inspector of naval ordnance. No mean feat.

Her features could only be described as placid; a smile hardly ever left her eyes, and to be alone, quietly, by the fire with her on a cold winter's evening, was to know an inner peace. Of this world's goods she never had much, but it never seemed to bother her. She had a very simple faith in God, and the fact (because to her it *was* a fact) that she didn't have much never worried her, because she knew that He would never let her reach rock-bottom. It was a simple faith of the kind that many who delve deep into theology seek and never achieve. When anyone condemned another to her, she would gently say, "My dear, if every one of us had our sins written across our forehead, not one of us would dare show our face outside the door."

She died as she had lived, peacefully and without fuss. In certain knowledge that she would be reunited with the husband she had never ceased to love, and face her Maker without fear.

She was the one to whom you could always turn. The one who always gave good advice. It was she who always knew how you felt, and knew how to cope. Fed you when you came in hungry, and warmed you when you were cold. The one who always understood and forgave- the one you could always trust. Her Maker may not have endowed her with material things, but he gave her so much else of great value. And like she did with everything else that she owned, she gladly gave it to others, and, not least, to me.

This then was my mother. Her life was dedicated to her family always, until her death thirty years ago. I, like many other sons, regret that I didn't always appreciate her as much as she deserved, and although at the time I could always come up with an excuse for not calling in for a second when I passed her door, there was never really any excuse good enough.

The last time I saw my mother was the afternoon before her death in hospital in the early hours of the following morning. Although she was very ill, we had no reason to believe that her death was imminent, but her whole demeanour told us that she no longer had the will to live, and she told us that she would soon be with Dad, and that she had seen him. Many years before, on the only other occasion that I had ever known her to be ill, she said that she had seen him and had been prepared to die then, but he put his hand out in a gesture to stop her, shook his head, and faded away. This time, she said that when he appeared he had beckoned to her. When I said to her that she mustn't talk like that, she said: "I'm not afraid to die. You two boys are all right and don't need me now; you have your families." I stayed with her until the end of the visiting time, kissed her, and told her that I would be in to see her the following day. But I was sure in my mind that I would not see her again. She died in the early hours of the morning. The night duty sister told me that she had done her rounds and found that Mum was sleeping peacefully. She had not had any sleeping tablets or anything of that nature, and when she again checked her she was no longer breathing. She slipped from sleep into death.

Many years ago, in 1941, when I was at the naval school, she had sent me an autograph book as a birthday present from my brother; we always gave each other presents, because there was only the three of us. Mum had put a little verse in.

A mother's love is a blessing,
Do not treat her with scorn,
Cherish her while she is living,
You will miss her when she is gone.

As usual, she was right.

Chapter Twenty-Two

My Father

I am surprised at the fact that, although I was a couple of months short of eleven years old when he lost his life, I remember so much about my father. Perhaps that is because he was a big man – not massive, but tall and solid. One of my earliest names for him was "Daddy-long-legs", and in the picture that I carry of him in my mind, he is nearly always in naval uniform. He was dark-haired, and had a good-natured face from which a smile was rarely very far; indeed, he was the sort of man one often found near the centre of a peal of laughter, and strangely enough, that is one of my earliest memories of him. His name was Archibald, and he was always known as Arch. During one of his spells away with the home fleet, my mother taught me an old music hall song. When he came home, Mother one day said to me, "Why don't you sing that song I taught you to Daddy?" I did, and if I remember the words correctly they went something like this:

"Why do they call me Archibald, Archibald, Archibald,
Why do they call me Archibald, I can't see.
A-R-C-H-I-E, that would be sufficient for me,
I don't mind them calling me Archie, but why the B-A-L-D?"

I can't remember ever seeing my dad laugh so much.

His childhood was, as it was with many others at that time, not one of plenty. He was one of a family of eight: four boys and four girls. My grandfather had been a merchant seaman, who had, I believe, suffered an injury at sea that had left him with a partly paralysed right arm, which in those times meant that there would be very poor prospects for employment. Consequently, my grandmother was the mainstay of the family, and took in washing to augment what little his father could earn.

As a consequence, all the boys had to start earning as soon as they could, and in a small seaside town like Dawlish there was not much in the way of career prospects. My father then started work as a baker's boy, a job which, although it didn't offer much in the way of a prospect for the future with regard to a career, did put him in the way of another kind of future, He met my mother. No, there is no wonderful romantic story about to unfold at this stage. My father left school at the age of twelve, and I believe was only about thirteen at this time. My mother was nearly three and a half years younger, and the daughter of the licensee of one of the local public houses. Her father had only recently died of consumption, and her mother had carried on at the Railway Inn.

Dad had been saving up for something that at that time was very dear to a boy's heart: fireworks. He had worked quite hard for this purpose, and the great day was near, but it was not to be. Mum came on the scene, running, not into his arms but nearly under the wheels of his delivery bike, which suffered enough damage to cost Dad his firework money. That was their first meeting, but thankfully not their last. From what Mum told me they did not really come together for some years, when my father was in the Navy, and Mum had become a nurse. This, then, was the beginning of a relationship which, although it was cut tragically short, gave my brother and me parents which, although perhaps could be equalled, could never be excelled.

According to my father's service records, he joined the Royal Navy in 1914, putting his age on by over a year, making his real age on enlistment seventeen. He served through the First World War, and was serving in HMS *Benbow*, one of Jellicoe's battleships at Jutland, and thereafter a succession of ships which kept him away for quite long periods of time.

He was a strict man in many senses and had been brought up in the Methodist tradition that Sunday was a day of rest, and that no manner of work should be undertaken apart from that which one had to do in the course of earning a living. As a child I remember Sundays being to us a day of purgatory. We were not allowed to go out to play and we were forbidden to play with any toys. We had to attend Sunday School, and the only form of amusement allowed was reading and perhaps games. If the weather was good, then a walk would relieve our boredom. I have thought about those Sundays since, and though I could never subscribe to such a rigid regime for Sundays, I can even now admire the principles that dictated it. He was a man of great principles which I never knew him to compromise. I remember that he had a really good tenor voice, and frequently sang solos in the chapel that he attended in St Budeaux, where they lived at the time; when I myself lived in the same neighbourhood forty years later, I met a lady with whom he had sung many duets.

He pensioned from the Navy in 1937, and the day that he finally left the service gave my mother a purse, with the crest of HMS *Drake*, the Royal Naval Barracks, containing a new half-crown, and said, "There you are. Now you'll never want for a meal while you've got that." I still have that purse. It has never been used, and still contains the half-crown, only it is not as pristine as the day he gave it to her. It is a piece of their life, which has always helped me to keep my feet on the ground.

Upon leaving the service, Dad took up his new job in London, as a postman attached to the Hendon district. He went back to night school, and passed the civil service examination in order to obtain a position in the Post Office side of the civil service, and it was not long before he took up his new post in the telegram service. He had made it, as he always wanted to, entirely by his own efforts. But fate intervened, and the war loomed. Mum tried to get him to apply to stay at home as being in a reserved occupation, and he almost certainly could have, but he would have none of it. He had a sense of duty which his principles would not allow him to shirk. Shortly after his death, a friend in the Post Office told my mother a story about Dad. He and Dad were walking back from their delivery round when Dad found a pound note on the pavement, and as the police station was almost next door to the office Dad went in to hand it over as lost property. His friend asked him why he hadn't kept it, and remarked that nobody would have known. My father replied "*I* would have known." He went on to say that when a policeman popped into their office to tell him that nobody had claimed it and that it was now his to claim, my father said, "Put it in the police orphan's box, it never was mine anyway." Such was the man, my father. To set such standards is to hand a son a great deal to live up to, and I am sure that there have been many times when I have fallen miserably short, and when at those times my conscience has bothered me, I can picture him saying, "Serves you right."

I think most of us have pictures in our minds of those that we have most loved, and who are no longer with us. I see my father mostly in naval uniform, but occasionally sitting in his special old armchair listening to the news on the new Murphy radio that he bought when we moved into the house that they had always longed and worked for. The other two visions I have of him are when we saw him off on the train to Portsmouth to go out to his ship in the China fleet, and the last time we said goodbye, and he stood waving from the platform of the bus taking him back to his ship which was moored alongside the breakwater, which left the following morning, to be sunk the following evening, and from which he never returned. I am positive that he never managed to get off the ship, because he was an extremely strong swimmer, and I know that he was on duty at the time that the torpedoes struck, and both the galleys where he worked, and his mess deck where he would have been if he had been off duty were deep in the ship. Because of the complete darkness below after the explosion, very few managed to get away. What I think is all the more tragic is that some years later, my mother told me he had once said to her, "There is something that I never told you all the time I was in the Navy, but I can now, and that is that I would never have liked to die from drowning." How cruel fate is. I still have the last letter that he wrote to me. We received it while we were still living in London and were about to come back to Plymouth where we saw him just a couple of times for a few hours. It had one of those silly pictures of his Ooslum bird town band, that lived on a diet of whalebone corsets and old iron bedsteads.

This then was my father. I loved him. He was fine man, and I have never known a better one. I missed him as a boy, and I still do. God bless him.

Chapter Twenty-Three

The Meeting

When I decided to research the sinking of *Courageous*, I examined my motives. Blame was not among them, unless we blame everyone who had failed to learn lessons from the past, and fate for conspiring to put together a sequence of coincidences that no human hand could have concocted. Any or all of these things could be blamed, but to do so would be a very futile exercise. The only conclusion that I could come to was that, try as I may, I could not rest until I knew all that it was possible to find out. It had haunted me through all the years, and even though I knew that whatever happened to come to light, it wouldn't make any difference, I still had to know. Now, today I do know all that happened as far as it is possible to find out after the intervening years, and I have at last laid the ghost that has haunted me until now.

I have always loved history and could never understand people who say that it is uninteresting. Probably one of the most stupid statements ever made about history was attributed to Henry T Ford when he said, "History is bunk". But the one that I think is most true is "Those who do not learn from the past are destined to relive it". Surely that must be true of the last two world conflicts.

It was with a little trepidation that I first contacted Kapt. Otto Schuhart, the commandant of U29. He was not too difficult to trace, but I did have misgivings, if that is the right word. I wanted an accurate picture of all the facts and events that led up to the sinking of *Courageous*, and it would not have been possible to achieve this without the help that he gave so freely,

I remember someone saying to me, "Why on earth do you want to meet the man who was responsible for sinking your father's ship?" I could not answer that. I only knew that I had to do this if it were possible. I also know that I could not look at the matter in that light.

My father was serving his country and doing his job... and so was Otto Schuhart.

I asked Schuhart, in my first letter to him, to describe his feelings at that time. His reply was, "You ask my sentiments. To say it briefly. I was a soldier and had to do my duty. I felt no enthusiasm for war, nor did I have sentiments of hate (perhaps a harsh word) towards my adversary. It was war; I loved my country and had to do my duty."

I cannot find any fault within that statement, although I have met those who have retorted, "Yes, they always say that 'I had to do my duty," and they made that their excuse." Well, I cannot go along with that view, and it certainly could not be applied to Schuhart. There are too many instances of his obvious humanity to his adversaries for there to be any doubts to the contrary. From the time that I contacted him, we corresponded for over seven years, and our letters covered all aspects of the sinking of *Courageous*, and the U-boat strategy over the whole period of the war. During this period, we tried to plan a meeting, but it seemed that everything conspired against it. The first time, Schuhart was away at a reunion at a time when I had to be in Germany, and on the second occasion his wife was taken ill and the visit had to be cancelled. What we did not know at the time was that his wife's illness was of a serious nature, and she would not recover. It was to be another two years before we were eventually to meet.

I often think that when something starts right, it is destined to continue in the same way; it was so in this case. Now, I am not exactly scared of flying, indeed, I had been flying on two previous occasions with my brother, who is qualified to fly light aircraft. Once in a Tiger Moth, and then in an Auster – and in a Tiger Moth the passenger sits in the front seat with the pilot behind him. My brother had tried to obtain a set of Gosport tubes, so that he could communicate with me during flight (these are rubber tubes which are plugged into the pilot's helmet mouthpiece and lead to the earpiece of the passenger's helmet, and work on the same principle as a stethoscope), but was unable to obtain any. However, he explained that as I was unable to fully turn round to look at him, and I would not be able to hear above the noise of the engine, he would have to tap me on the shoulder to point things out. I can still remember sitting in the front seat, rumbling along the field to take off, suddenly no longer feeling the wheels rumbling and finding that we were airborne, and hoping that he was still in the back seat! After a while, feeling a tap on my shoulder every minute or two when he pointed out various landmarks in and around Plymouth, feeling reassured that he was still there, I settled down to try and enjoy my first flight.

I had, however, never travelled by jet, and on the morning that we boarded the Lufthansa flight to Stuttgart I was to say the least a tiny little bit apprehensive. On boarding the aircraft, we were given a choice of either of two newspapers to read on the flight. One was a German paper, I believe it was the *Frankfurter Allgemeiner*, and the other *The Sunday Times*. I chose the *Times*. We took off along the runway and rose like a rocket, leaving my stomach and peace of mind behind.

It was a gloriously sunny day in late August, and there wasn't a cloud in the sky all the way from London to Stuttgart. I had by now a feeling of fatalism with regard to flying. I had left the ground and was in the air, travelling, I was told by the captain, at over five hundred knots, and at a height of thirty-odd thousand feet, and the air temperature outside was, I think he said, fifty below zero. I sat back and settled down to read. I took *The Sunday Times* magazine from the pocket at the back of the seat. I have often thought of getting a bookmaker or an insurance actuary to quote me the odds against what happened next. On the front page of the magazine there was a picture of a passenger jet, and the caption saying, "Planes that fall to pieces, pilots that fall asleep, and controllers who cannot cope. Is flying becoming too dangerous?" There followed accounts of pieces of passenger jets found at strategic points on many of the world's main routes, tales of pilots so fatigued that they had been found asleep by stewardesses visiting the flight deck, and air-traffic controllers who had freaked out, leaving the room with aircraft stacked awaiting landing instructions! I still have that magazine.

I can honestly say that flying does not frighten me, although I have to admit that the prospect does not fill me with unbounded joy. I am well aware that all statistics say that, balanced against other forms of travel it has an enviable safety record, but, once in the air, should anything happen, then the chances of coming out of any incident alive are not rated as being as high as they would be in any other normal form of transport. No, in my humble opinion, the only civilised forms of transport are by rail, on land, and to travel away from these shores, the sea. But the fact of the coincidence of taking one's first jet flight and within ten minutes of take-off reading such an article appealed to my at times wayward sense of humour, and this, certainly like all humour, put me in the right frame of mind to approach my first meeting with Kapt. Schuhart.

My wife and I had travelled up overnight from Plymouth to take the flight to Stuttgart, and were rather tired by the time we landed. During the flight I found myself wondering what the first meeting between Kapt. Schuhart and myself would be like. We had carried on a long correspondence, and I had built up a mental picture of him from this, and eventually found that this picture was fairly accurate. His letters were always fairly formal but always courteous, and as we progressed, friendly. I pictured an officer of the old Imperial German Navy school, precise, thorough, and meticulous.

When we arrived at his residence and rang the bell, it was a little time before the door opened. When it did, I asked, "Kapitan Schuhart?" His reply was, "*Herzlich Willkommen.*" The weather, as I have said, was extremely hot, and what with the long coach journey overnight and the wait for our flight, my wife was more than a little jaded, and once we were inside and had dropped our bag Schuhart immediately turned to her and said, "Mrs Gibbings, you would like some refreshment." It was more a statement than a question. She replied, "Oh, yes please, I would love a cup of—" She got no further. "I know," he interjected, "tea." He paused, "But I only drink coffee." He paused again, then, seeing the slightly disappointed look on my wife's face, went on, smiling, "But I bought some tea for you yesterday." This then was the start of a meeting which I thought at the time might have begun with at least a little feeling of awkwardness and intrusion on my part, but my fears were groundless.

It was only a very short time before we felt at ease and our conversation turned to the main purpose of our visit. I feel sure that the fact that we had both had a service background made things much easier for us. I had planned a course for my many questions to take, but it soon became obvious that it was better to let our conversations range and follow where they led. This very soon proved to be wise.

We very soon agreed that the whole concept of sending out fleet carriers to hunt submarines was, to say the least, unwise, and had been proved to be so within fourteen days of the declaration of war, when *Ark Royal* had so nearly fallen victim to U39, and *Courageous* had become a victim three days later.

The *Ark Royal* would very probably have fallen victim if the captain of U39 had heeded Schuhart's warning two days earlier, when he had sunk the *Neptunia* with the old impact torpedoes after failing to do so with the new magnetic type.

Some time after the war Schuhart had met up again with the captain of U39 and had asked him why he had not taken notice of his warning. It appears that he didn't seem to know the answer himself.

From the *Ark Royal* incident we went on to his operations from the time that he had arrived at his patrol area, which were covered earlier, and from there to the lead up to the sighting of *Courageous* in the afternoon of 17th September. It was strange that Schuhart knew absolutely nothing about the attack of the U53 on the *Kafiristan* after all those years. I had heard many years before that the calling away of the *Inglefield* and *Intrepid* was a deliberate decoy attempt, but I am sure that this only stemmed from the fact that by pure coincidence; the same thing happened in the case of *Ark Royal*, when she detached *Tartar*, *Bedouin*, and *Punjab* to go to the assistance of the SS *Fanad Head*, which had been attacked by a U-boat about 180 miles to the south-west, and was herself attacked shortly after, albeit unsuccessfully, by U39. For the same thing to happen in so short a space of time, three days, must at the time have seemed to be more than coincidence, but it nevertheless was.

I do know that Schuhart thought that it was rather strange that such a valuable prize as a fleet carrier was at sea in such a dangerous area with an escort of only two destroyers. Prize is the right word, for she was almost handed to him on a plate. He could hardly believe his luck, but who could blame him for capitalising on it?

I mentioned that at the time of the sinking there had been several reports that his boat had been seen after the attack and that several men had reported that it had been blown to the surface and definitely destroyed. He replied that on firing the torpedoes he had dived to sixty metres. They had heard the explosions, but at no time did they even come up for a look. Wise man!

Chapter Twenty-Four

Plymouth

It has been said, that for its size and population, Plymouth was the most heavily bombed city in the country. There can be no doubt that it suffered horrendously, both in terms of casualties and structural damage. Almost overnight the heart was torn out of her and she lost many of her people. Before the Blitz was over, many of her families had lost their homes twice. But she was never defeated. She was a garrison town, and a seaport, and her people were made of stern stuff. So she picked herself up, spat out the dust, licked her wounds, and got on with the job of winning. Her dockyard worked ceaselessly, day and night, and her armament factories did the same; it never occurred to them to do otherwise. They didn't feel sorry for themselves; they didn't get mad, they got even. Then the war ended, although there was a time when they thought that it never would, but it did, and they stopped to draw breath, and looked around, and at last had time to take full stock. It was a stocktaking that didn't take long, because there wasn't so much left to take stock of. There was a lot of rubble, and a few makeshift nissen hut shops, and shored-up old buildings, and many war-worn weary people who had very little left but plain old-fashioned guts. True, there were a few short moments when they weren't quite sure whether they wanted a wash, shave, shampoo or haircut, because they had been so long getting on with it, that it was sort of strange when it had all stopped, and, like bailing out a leaky boat, suddenly there was no longer any water left to bail.

After realising that at last it was all over, we turned our minds to the future, to find that for some little time a group of people had already been planning it. We were the first city to start replanning, and if anything good can be said about the destruction at all, it is that the devastation was so complete that it left us with almost a clear area with hardly anything left that could stand in the way of a design for a lovely new city. Our guildhall had suffered heavy damage, but there was sufficient left standing for us to repair and rebuild it, as a reminder to future generations of the best of our old city and its past. The only regret that I personally have is not that a new Plymouth was built - it deserved to be - but that my dear old Devonport was in my opinion sacrificed to make it possible. Granted, Devonport was part of Plymouth in that it was, with Stonehouse, amalgamated to form the City of Plymouth, but the sad thing was that it sacrificed its own identity in the process. The rubble was cleared away from Devonport, but it was many years before the bomb sites were no longer there to remind us of her suffering. Devonport still has scars; her beautiful park was cut in two by a road, but I still go there at times, and stand and look out over the Hamoaze, remembering the days when dozens of ships would be moored there when the home fleet came in after exercises, and the town that night would be packed with sailors.

There has never been a time when the Royal Navy has not had a presence in Plymouth; indeed, it is not possible to think of one without the other, and, of course, in this context one must include HM Dockyard. It is true to say that the Royal Navy and the dockyard have until recent years provided the mainstay of employment, not only for the whole city of Plymouth, but for an area far beyond the city limits, indeed stretching for a very considerable distance into Cornwall. While for generations it has provided a very stable and secure working future for many thousands, it has always had a very definite disadvantage, in that this has resulted in one of the lowest wage structures anywhere in the United Kingdom. The people of Plymouth have always been very aware of this, and while they have from time to time protested against this inescapable fact, successive governments of all political colours have quite deliberately completely ignored such protests; indeed it has always been in the interests of successive governments to discourage the setting up of any viable alternative industries, as this would have given the workforce an alternative to the defence-orientated industries, and thereby increased the wage bill by reason of the competition that would have resulted. But despite this, the people of Plymouth have always made the best of a bad job; very probably because there was very little that they could do about it. Over the years, generations of young apprentices learned their trades in 'The Yard'. It has always been recognised that there was no better place to learn a trade. Any man who could produce evidence of having learned his trade in HM Dockyard could rely on the fact that his qualifications were recognised and respected anywhere. The only problem was that outside the dockyard there were no other firms in the area that required the undoubted skills that these men had.

The result of this state of affairs is that over the years, as the decline of the Navy continued, there has been a gradual worsening of the situation until it has reached crisis point. Plymouth, has been more sadly neglected by government policy with regard to all forms of aid than any other industrial declining area in the country, and there is no excuse for this neglect, although there are reasons if one looks far enough. These reasons are political, in that other similar areas that have suffered industrial decline have, for a variety of reasons, been able to exert more political pressure by dint of their geographical or commercial importance. One factor in the south-west is that the number of Members of Parliament for the area covered by Devon and Cornwall is quite small compared with other areas of industrial decline, e.g. South Yorkshire, and the population is concentrated in just a few centres.

The loyalty and dedication of the workforce in the dockyard and all the many other defence-orientated workplaces in the south-west has never wavered. During the war, the tempo of work never altered, and as recently as the Falklands conflict, the yard, although it had even at that time been run down to only a fraction of its old capacity, performed prodigious feats of production, repair and maintenance well within the time limits that were expected of them, or indeed had been thought possible. However, the rundown of the defence industries as a whole at this present point time has been so severe that it is almost impossible to believe that the same performance could be repeated.

During the last war the strength of the Royal Navy stood at something like 500,000 men, and the number of ships could be assessed on the basis that even with that number of men, there were never enough to man them all even with the shore support of the WRNS. It must therefore follow that after the war ended there would have to be an almost immediate need to reduce that number drastically to say the least. That need was satisfied by the phased demobilisation of hostilities-only men, and the run-down progressed as ships were withdrawn from service due to obsolescence and many others over a period of time being surplus to requirements. At this stage there was no great problem as good old 'natural wastage' seemed to be doing a good job. Then, came the cold war, and Korea, and a drastic rethink was necessary, and to compound the problem the advent of advanced electronic and nuclear warfare made both the problems and solutions very much more difficult. Then there was the final factor. Government demanded more savings in defence expenditure to meet the ever-growing demands of the Welfare State, and these savings were needed urgently.

It does not require a genius to see that the greater the urgency for cuts, the less likely it is that a sensible and well-planned defence strategy is likely to follow, and therefore the ill-conceived hotchpotch of the latest round of cuts is the natural corollary of this.

One of the most blatant of the mistakes was made in the mid fifties, when a large slice of Devonport was walled off and taken into the dockyard, and this at a time when we were reducing the size of the Navy. Sensible planning could surely have coped. If we had managed to cope during the war, albeit with difficulty, and to get by with the dockyard the size that it was at that time, then, with the will to do so, it would have been possible to have managed at a time when the size of the Navy, and the maintenance requirement was less, and still shrinking. Although it may appear to be a bit of oversimplification, it is difficult to imagine a shopkeeper increasing the size of his premises at a time when his business is on the decrease, with no plans to expand it.

There can be very little doubt that Plymouth has been very shabbily treated by successive governments, and to date, there seems to be no move towards remedying the situation. The south-west in general always seems to be behind the door when any national goodies are up for grabs. It could be said that if there was a famine and it rained soup, the government would see to it that Plymouth would be issued with a fork with which to collect it. It is time that there was a change in government attitude to the south-west as a whole and Plymouth in particular, a city that has served the country well and loyally over generations, toiling away at the only large industry that she had. Now that is gone, and although she has made valiant efforts to encourage new industry, particularly embracing all the new technologies, and is trying hard even now to increase tourism and the holiday industry, it is not enough. We need more help and funding, but not funding alone, although that is important. The people of

Plymouth have never waited for someone to feed them and give them handouts, it is not in their nature. All they require is what these days is called a level playing field, a government approach that will take into account what she has achieved and what she has given to the country, and the Navy in particular. This is the city, which, because of its strategic importance in the war, was, for its size, the most heavily bombed city in the country, and proportionate to its population, suffered the greatest number of civilian causalities – 1073. It is time for the government to pay its debts.

Chapter Twenty-Five

Damage Limitation

After the First World War it was no longer necessary to maintain a large standing army and navy, and for some time there was a steady reduction by demobilisation and natural wastage. In 1923 the findings of the Geddes Report resulted in a massive reduction in manpower in the Royal Navy, which, coupled with the implementation of the Washington naval treaty, reduced the service to a level that indicated to any potential enemy that, taking into account the worldwide commitments of the nation at that time, we would be too thinly stretched to be able to adequately defend the Empire and homeland, and keep the sea lanes open for the import of food and materials.

This situation was interpreted by Hitler as unwillingness to do anything tangible to frustrate his territorial ambition, whereas a sensible and gradual upgrading of our defences would have given a clear signal that we were not prepared to give him a free hand in Europe. The result of this neglect was the unnecessary loss of ships which were not suitable for the tasks that they were given, and the death of many men. This in turn was largely due to the fact that many were recalled pensioners and reservists who were too old to cope with life-threatening situations at sea, or, in the case of reservists, not adequately trained.

There is no need to go further into the damage inflicted on the armed services in general, and the Royal Navy in particular, by all the cuts inflicted over recent years. Suffice it to say, they have been far too many and far too deep, and what is more important is that there must not be any more. History itself has shown us the consequences of this folly, and there are people still alive who bear the scars. The fact is that there are those in responsible positions in this country who have yet to learn how to strike a balance between keeping a strong and viable navy, capable of dealing with situations such as the Falkland

Islands and Gulf War, and sensible elimination of waste and over-capacity - something that, up till now, seems to have been beyond the ability of the authors of recent defence cuts. The lack of foresight is instanced in the case of the closure of the Royal Naval Engineering College at Manadon in Plymouth, a centre of international excellence which we will never be able to re-establish. This was indeed an act of almost criminal vandalism. It was said that it was a more economic proposition to train all naval engineers at civilian universities. Private industry has complained for some time of the lack of trained engineers and the lack of training facilities, and then we destroy the finest training facility in this country for both engineering and electronics. Did it not occur to those responsible that Manadon could have been used to train civilians as well as service personnel, and could also have taken overseas students? The MOD would have been paid to do so, thus making it a viable proposition.

I attended the sale of all the machinery and equipment at the RNEC at Manadon, and it was heartbreaking to see the many millions of pounds worth of equipment sold off for a fraction of what it cost the taxpayer, knowing that it will never be possible to replace it.

It would be possible to continue with the catalogue of waste and folly, but that would be a futile exercise. It is better to try and convince those responsible, if possible, to find more sensible ways to reduce the burden of defence expenditure by perhaps releasing more MOD land and property to the cities in which they are situated, so that the authorities could use them instead of having to find other space and premises for trade, commerce and industry, thereby creating more employment and housing, and adding to local economies which have suffered so much from having been tied to the defence, naval and military industries for so many centuries. It is my sincere hope that this plea will be heard by those whose task is to shape our defence for the future, and that they will seriously consider a different approach - but judging on past performance, I will not hold my breath.

Another factor that seems not to have been given any great amount of thought is that it is possible to train civilians in parallel with service personnel in many disciplines. In years gone by, service training in many areas, while thorough - and indeed in many cases far more comprehensive - did not result in a qualification that was of use or indeed recognised in civilian life, But that is not so now. Most service training is geared to lead to the same qualifications required for life after the service. It therefore follows that there is a sound argument for using many of the training facilities for training civilians. This would lead to a pool of very highly skilled technicians and artisans, who, although they might not wish to enter the armed services, would obtain qualifications which would enhance their employment prospects in industry, thereby remedying a situation which has long been complained of by the leaders of industry in this country: that there is a dearth of facilities for the training of the engineers and technicians which they say our industries need.

The argument is put forward that this would not be as simple as it sounds, and perhaps there is a grain of truth in this, but we all know that government can do anything it wishes if it has the political will. If it really is the policy of government to remedy the shortage of training capacity, then here is the opportunity. Make use of all the service training capacity available, and you not only achieve the goal of providing training capacity for private industry for which a charge could be made, but you remove the need to close down service facilities on the grounds of economy. This would then leave very valuable defence assets intact, and for once allow us to have our cake and eat it.

It is still not too late. Granted, it will be a case of just in time, and only just, but better that than to make that last cut; the one that we will not recover from – our throat.

Criticism is a bad thing if it is only destructive, and there is a real necessity to now offer a more constructive approach. If a system is working well, then there is no reason to alter it – if it ain't broke, don't fix it – but in this case it *does* need fixing, because it is patently obvious that it is not working. So, let's go back to the drawing board.

To summarise:

1. The first consideration should be, what the real defence needs of the nation are, bearing in mind that situations can change very rapidly.
2. Defence is *too* important and complicated to be left to ordinary politicians, who more often than not have no real concept of the relevance of history, which should always be considered and applied in the study of global and national defence. Too many politicians in the past have been entrusted with defence decisions, and have only the sketchiest knowledge of history (one of the world's greatest teachers) and little or no knowledge of the

services and their thinking processes. By the same token, it cannot be entirely left to high-ranking service officers, who are often influenced by a genuine desire to fight their own corner, and sometimes by the thought, that making the wrong noises will ensure that they will be the victims of the next round of cuts.

3. A clear distinction should be made between cuts and economies, which by definition are not related.
4. Far more thought and consideration should be given to the effect that any changes could have on the morale of servicemen and women; a matter which up to now has not been given the importance that it deserves. Recent recruiting attempts have been found to be suffering because, after a period of cuts throughout the services, young people no longer looked on the services as a long-term employment option in the same way as they did in the past.
5. Arguments that the threat of global conflict have receded since the collapse of the former Soviet Union are to say the least, spurious, and one only has to consider that a change in leadership in that part of the globe could probably completely alter the situation; to say nothing of the fact that two of the worlds most unstable regimes, Iraq and Iran, almost certainly have a nuclear capability, as has China. When other commitments such as fishery protection, search and rescue, security of dependencies (Falkland Islands), Customs and Excise, and policing of gun-running and drugs smuggling is considered, then a navy of the present strength of under 42,000 officers and ratings could not even begin to cope adequately.
6. Awareness of the effect of constructive accountancy on the minds of those having to make decisions regarding economies is an important factor. Constructive accountancy is the art of taking a simple matter like the journey of an individual from A to B, which in the normal course of events would cost £10, and by applying certain little tricks of the trade, like how many times the individual would pay a visit to the loo on the journey, and the cost of admittance; allowing for delays and the consequent need to obtain sustenance, and allowing for the cleaning of clothes worn on the journey, thereby increasing the £10 to a figure resembling the national debt.

Finally, while it is common sense to economise, it is pointless to do so to the extent that the services cannot any longer cope with the very tasks which are their whole reason for being. If you want a tree to thrive and bear fruit, you don't take an axe to it. You prune it… gently!

Chapter Twenty-Six

We Who Broke Faith

Whenever I visit a village or town in England, I can never stop and look at a war memorial without wondering about the men whose names are inscribed on it. I find myself wondering what course those lives would have taken if they had survived, and what they would have achieved. There is no doubt that the vast majority would have lived their lives out just earning a living, as do the majority of ordinary people. But that is not the point. I recall some verse by Housman:

Here dead lie we because we did not choose
To live and shame the land from which we sprung.
Life, to be sure, is nothing much to lose;
But young men think it is, and we were young.

I also think of another quote that I have read somewhere.

The greatest sacrifice of all, is the gift of an unfinished life.

War has ever been a waste, and utterly futile; the nadir of man's failure. It is a waste of human life. It is a waste of material, and finally, it is a waste of opportunity, in that going to war brings out both the best and worst in the human race, but avoiding war, and settling differences by diplomacy and negotiation, brings out only the best.

Among the dead were the people who would perhaps have cured cancer, or become the great philosophers, or another Shakespeare, Elgar, Coward, Churchill, Wren, or become a great statesman. We will never know. What an appalling waste, and it need not have been. For each name on the memorial there are many more lives that followed a different course because that name is there. I have known many of these stories - indeed, I was one of them, and even now wonder what different course my life would have taken had my father's name not been inscribed on a war memorial. Then, I wonder, if, after all the intervening years, those men could return and see how the world had changed, and what they would think of our stewardship.

I wonder what they would think of the lowering of standards; the drug culture; the increase in violent crime and greed; the increase in business fraud which largely goes unpunished, and even when it is, the perpetrators getting sentences which make a mockery of the judicial system, and then getting early release to again head businesses; divorce laws which are so lax as to endorse little better than legal prostitution; homosexuality, which in their lifetime was punishable by imprisonment, but which now by the action of liberal-minded do-gooders has come to be accepted and encouraged, to the extent which makes one wonder how long it will be before it is made compulsory; sheer wanton vandalism for no reason; the widespread bloodsucking of the nation's wealth via the Welfare State and the awarding of vast sums of money in compensation to people who have suffered so called trauma while doing the job they contracted to do in the first place.

The list is endless, and is a blot on the nation's conscience. It could be argued that many of the men alive now who survived that awful war did come home and over the years have been guilty of many of the things mentioned since those times; that they changed over the years and let their standards slip, but, by and large I think that the family unit and the general moral code by which families were brought up in those times would make that the exception rather than the rule.

One thing that is quite certain about the last world conflict that was different from the First World War is that it was obvious to most people that the world was never going to be the same again. A whole era had ended, and a new one was beginning, but even making allowances for the changes that every generation has to accept, I cannot believe that we should have accepted some of the new morality which we have, to say the least, allowed to enter into our national character.

It is true that we can point to many faults in the morality of bygone days, but never on such a massive scale as we see now, and certainly such behaviour was never accepted as the norm, and indeed encouraged as in today's society. In this respect we have indeed broken faith with our war dead.